An easy-to-follow tourists' guide

D1297536

D-Day

and the

Liberation of Normandy

1944

Brian Olof

AN EASIGUIDES PUBLICATION

ACKNOWLEDGEMENTS

Thanks are due:
to the authors and publishers of the books noted in the Appendix for many of the historical and other facts used in this booklet, particularly to John Keegan and Major Tonie Holt; to the Ville de Caen, Normandy, and the Imperial War Museum for the use of the photographs; to Gaye Briscoe (of Type 24, Petersfield) for typing the manuscript; to Brenda Drummond for the typographical artwork; to Marc Hendriks and his colleagues for help in using Lotus Freelance to draw the maps; to the people, too many to name, who have provided help and advice in the production of this guide - and to Dennis Church for the idea.

First published May, 1993
Reprinted September, 1993
Reprinted March, 1994

Published by EASIGUIDES
72 Froxfield Green, Petersfield, Hampshire GU32 1DQ,
England
Telephone: 0730-262447

© 1993 Brian Olof
ISBN 0 9520398 0 X

British Library Catologuing-in-Publication Data.
A catalogue record for this book is
available from the British Library.

Copyright reserved. No part of this publication may be reproduced, stored in a retrieval system, or transmitted, in any form or by any means, electronic, mechanical, photocopying, recording or otherwise, without the prior permission of the copyright owner.

INTRODUCTION

Many books have been written on the subject of the liberation of Normandy by the Allied forces in June 1944, but most of them deal with the political aspects and the military strategy which are fascinating to some, but of little interest to most passing tourists.

There are also a few good guide books on the subject, but these usually go into greater detail than can be absorbed by the casual visitor.

This booklet, however, is aimed at those tourists who just want to see where it happened and read a very basic story at each site to help them get some feeling for the achievements and tragedies of this famous battle. It is hoped that, in so doing, they will remember those, both military and civilian, who died or were wounded in the cause of freedom.

CONTENTS

WE WILL REMEMBER THEM

This guide is dedicated to all those who fought for the liberation of Normandy and to the people of France who bore so much during the battle.   In particular, it is dedicated to the memory of those who died and to those, many still alive today, who suffered the physical and mental scars of war.

For every book sold, a contribution will be made to The Royal Star & Garter Home for Disabled Sailors, Soldiers & Airmen.   Several Normandy Veterans live there. A further sum will be donated to the Union Départmentale des Combattants Volontaires de la Résistance du Calvados.

The Royal Star and Garter Home stands high on Richmond Hill in the west of London overlooking the River Thames.   Although it first opened its doors in 1916, today's Home provides the very latest equipment and standards of medical and nursing care.   Any physically disabled man and woman who has served with Her Majesty's regular or reserve forces may apply for a place, regardless of rank, age, length of service or cause of disability.

The Royal Star and Garter Home, Richmond, Surrey TW10 6RR
Registered charity numbers 210119 and 286781

The Association of Resistance Volunteers in the Department of Calvados keeps alive the memory of those French civilians whose brave acts of sabotage helped so much in the liberation of their homeland.   The Association's aims are to care for its Veterans and to pass on their spirit of patriotism to future generations.

MAPS

PHOTOGRAPHS

By kind permission of the Ville de Caen, Normandy #
and The Trustees of the Imperial War Museum, London ##

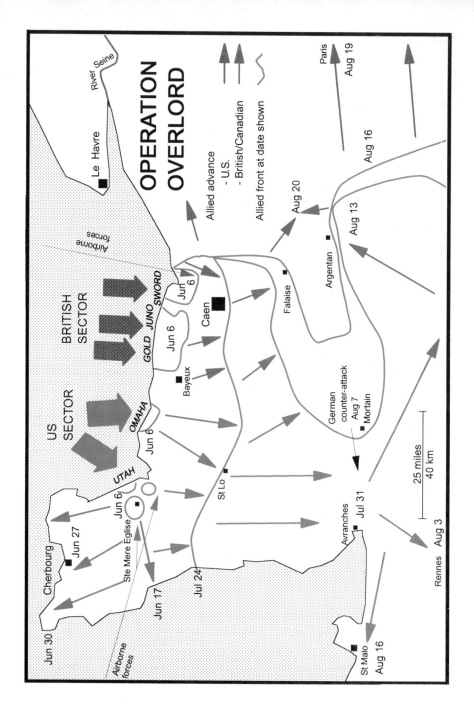

OPERATION OVERLORD

Allied advance
- U.S.
- British/Canadian
Allied front at date shown

River Seine
Le Havre
Airborne forces
BRITISH SECTOR
SWORD
JUNO
GOLD
Jun 6
Jun 6
Caen
Bayeux
US SECTOR
OMAHA
Jun 6
UTAH
Jun 6
Ste Mere Eglise
Airborne forces
Cherbourg
Jun 27
Jun 30
Jun 17
Jul 24
St Lo
Avranches
Jul 31
Rennes
Aug 3
St Malo
Aug 16
Mortain
German counter-attack
Aug 7
Falaise
Argentan
Aug 13
Aug 20
Aug 16
Paris
Aug 19
25 miles
40 km

OVERVIEW

Soon after Britain declared war on Germany on 3rd September 1939, following the German invasion of Poland, forces of the British Commonwealth landed in France. In late May 1940, they were overwhelmed by the German army and those who were not killed or captured managed a miraculous escape from Dunkirk. A huge fleet, ranging in size from ferries to dinghies, crossed again and again from the English coast to rescue 225,000 troops.

The United States entered the war on 7th December 1941 when the Japanese made a devastating attack on the U.S. fleet in Pearl Harbor in Hawaii. The Allies were now powerful enough to start planning the liberation of Europe against the mighty defences of the Germans which were constantly growing in strength along the entire length of the French coast bordering the Atlantic and the English Channel (see page 85). In August 1942, 5,000 Canadians tested the German fortifications at Dieppe. In spite of their great skill and bravery, it was a disastrous failure, resulting in 900 men being killed and over 2,400 being wounded or captured.

The landings on and after D-Day, known as "Operation Overlord", were the greatest ever in the history of warfare. Under the supreme command of General Eisenhower (based at Southwick House outside Portsmouth), they began with airborne landings by paratroops and gliders - in all, 23,000 men - soon after midnight on the morning of 6th June 1944. The Americans landed around Ste. Mère Eglise at the bottom of the Cherbourg peninsula and the British to the east of the canal and river running from Caen to the sea. These landing zones were at either end of the intended landing beaches so that German reinforcements could be held at bay. The sea transportation, code-named "Operation Neptune", was massive with over 7,000 vessels being used to carry, or to support, over 150,000 men. They started landing, in heavy seas, from 6.30 a.m. - the Americans at "Utah" and "Omaha" beaches in the west and the British at "Gold", "Juno" (Canadians) and "Sword" to the east.

The aim of the operation was for the British sector, under the command of General Montgomery, to keep the German tanks occupied around Caen, whilst the Americans, led by General Bradley, captured the Cherbourg peninsula, then turned south. Joined by a third army (under General Patton), they would swing east around the British and then all the Allies would drive the Germans back across the Seine into Germany. By late August all this was achieved, but in the process a huge force of 100,000 Germans was caught in a pocket between Falaise and Argentan, south of Caen. 50,000 Germans escaped through the mouth of the pocket but 10,000 were killed and 40,000 were captured.

Normandy had been liberated!

HOW TO USE THIS BOOKLET

There are twelve MAIN TOURS lettered A to L.   Within each main tour there is a BASIC tour and a FULL tour.   Each of these 24 tours follows a number of self-contained MODULES.   Each tour takes these modules in a different order, so the modules end with LINKS which lead you to your next module (or back to your main tour).

BASIC OR FULL TOUR?

Before choosing your main tour, decide whether you want a BASIC or a FULL tour. This depends on your level of interest in the subject and the time you have available. At this stage decide on your level of interest.   On page 10 there is a list of the modules covered by all BASIC tours and another list of those additional modules that are included in the FULL tours.   The BASIC tours are all north of, or close to, the N13 road from Cherbourg to Caen and cover the D-Day landing beaches and air drop zones, with plenty of museums and other sites to visit.   They also visit Bayeux which has an excellent museum covering the Normandy battles after D-Day, with the opportunity of seeing the city.   The other museums cover the local events of D-Day itself and there is little repetition.

The FULL tours are an extension of the basic tours and visit additional areas where battles took place during the two and a half months after D-Day.   Their interest depends largely on the imagination of the visitor, assisted by the battle descriptions in each module and on the plaques of several monuments.   They include visits to museums at Caen and Falaise, as well as an optional tour of the city of Caen.

DETOUR OR SPECIAL VISIT?

You should now select your main tour A to L.   These are listed on page 1 and there is an area map on page 112, followed by a map for each tour.   Your choice depends on whether you plan to see the area on the way to or from another holiday to be taken further south, or make a special visit.   You can, of course, just follow one or more modules independently.

If you're on the way elsewhere you should follow one of the DETOURS (Tours A to F) depending on your port of arrival or departure.   Visitors from the Channel Islands and those who wish to cross the channel via the Tunnel or to any of the ports from Le Havre to Calais should read the special notes on page 105.

You must decide whether to take the tour at the beginning of your holiday ("going south") or at the end ("going north").   If you have no firm plans, one of the detours going south is recommended as they generally follow the direction of the

Allied advance.   This might not concern you but it makes the battle stories easier
to understand and hopefully more interesting.

SPECIAL VISITS

HOW MANY HOURS IN A DAY?
Most people will catch an overnight ferry in both directions.   You will arrive in
France about 7 a.m. and assuming you will wish to reach your overnight
accommodation by 6 p.m., this will give you nine touring hours (having allowed
two hours for lunch, coffee etc.).   On your last day, you will leave your
accommodation about 9 a.m. and will probably want to arrive at a restaurant by 8
p.m., giving your plenty of time for the late night sailing.   That's another nine
touring hours.   On middle days, you will have from 9 a.m. until 6 p.m., giving
you only seven touring hours.   On a one-day trip you have from 7 a.m. until 8
p.m. or eleven hours, though this can be extended to twelve or more by having a
quick sandwich lunch and no stops for coffee.

So, on a 1 day visit, you have 11 hours (plus) available, 2 days - 18 hours, 3 days -
25 hours, 4 days - 32 hours, 5 days - 39 hours and 6 days - 46 hours.   The special
tours are estimated to take the following time [hours:minutes]:-

			BASIC	FULL
G	Circular	- Cherbourg	23:05	36:10
H		- Caen	20:55	33:25
I		- St. Malo	25:25	40:05
J	Cherbourg to Caen		21:15	35:10
K	Caen to St. Malo		22:50	37:05
L	Cherbourg to St. Malo		24:00	38:05

In practice you may find that you will be quicker than these times (see Timings later
in this section), though they **exclude** taking the opportunity to glimpse at Bayeux (15
mins) or Caen (1 hr) or to spend a half-day in the former or a day in the latter -
both recommended.   If you are travelling through St. Malo there is also that town
to see, as well as Le Mont St. Michel.

BASIC TOURS
If you can spare only one day for the tour, you should follow the beginning and the
end of Basic Tour H, a circular tour from Ouistreham, leaving out Utah, Ste Mère
and Bayeux modules - see the separate section on page 22.   If you have only two
days, with careful planning and one eye on the clock you should be able to complete
the whole of Basic Tour H.

It will be far better, however, if you could allow three days for a basic tour - or longer if you wish to extend your visits to any of the museums or see more of the towns.   H or J would be best, depending on your choice of home ferry port.   H is the one recommended for visitors coming in to Ouistreham (with Brittany Ferries through Portsmouth), to ports further east or from the Channel Tunnel.   J is for those wishing to travel with P&O, arriving at Cherbourg and ending with a drive from Caen to Le Havre which takes less than two hours - both ways through Portsmouth.   In season, Brittany Ferries have a service to Cherbourg from Poole and you can return to Portsmouth from Ouistreham.   Circular G is similar to H but is for those wishing to base their tour on Cherbourg (Brittany Ferries from Poole, P&O Ferries from Portsmouth or Stena Sealink from Southampton).

Tours I, K and L involve more driving as they end in St. Malo, but you will see more of the Normandy countryside this way, with the opportunity of visiting the famous Mont St. Michel as well as St. Malo itself.   K from Ouistreham is the shortest (225 miles) and has the advantage of starting and finishing at Portsmouth. L from Cherbourg is 30 miles longer and means leaving from Poole and returning to Portsmouth (presuming you wish to travel both ways with the same ferry company, in this case, Brittany Ferries).   Tour I (St. Malo circular) should be chosen for the basic tour if you need to start and end in St. Malo, but it is quite a long drive (335m).

FULL TOURS
All the full tours take five days, though this can be shortened to four (especially H and J and possibly G) by watching the clock, by omitting a module or by cutting down (or cutting out) a museum visit.   They could also take longer if you wish to spend more time in museums or cemeteries or go into Bayeux, Caen, Mont St. Michel or St. Malo - all recommended.

The same considerations apply to the various alternative tours as with the basic tours.   Not all of them cover the Cobra module as it is somewhat off most routes, but if you want to see real "bocage" country (see page 46) you can easily make a detour.

HOW TO FOLLOW THE CHOSEN TOUR
Turn to the page for your chosen tour (A to L, BASIC or FULL).   You will see the distance you will need to drive, the estimated time required for travelling and the minimum time recommended for visits to sites of interest.   The basis for these times is explained in "Timings" below.

If you are timing the tour to arrive at a port to catch a particular ferry, you may be concerned to know how much more time is needed to complete the tour. On each main tour page you will see two columns headed "Time (hr:min)". The left column is the time estimated to complete the module named on that line plus the link appropriate to that particular tour. The right column is the time needed to complete the tour, after the module on its left has been completed. If time is running low, you could cut short a museum visit (or cut it out altogether) or even leave out a complete module - this is where a map will come in handy - Michelin map No. 231 "Normandie" to the scale 1:200,000 is recommended.

Having chosen a tour, it is vital that you remember its code letter and whether it is BASIC or FULL as these guide you from module to module (e.g. "BASIC L" or "FULL B". "TOUR C" includes BASIC C and FULL C).

TIMINGS

The times suggested in this booklet are based on the time taken by the author in surveying the routes. As this was done in January, 20% has been added to allow for holiday season congestion. Travel times also include minor stops, for example to read a memorial, and time to allow solo drivers to read the narrative. There is a lot of mileage to cover, with many stops, so journeys were driven at or near to the speed limits, i.e. 68 mph (110 kph) on dual carriageways and 56 mph (90 kph) on other roads. In towns (starting with the town sign and ending with a sign with a bar across the name) the limit is 31 mph (50 kph).

Times given for visits to museums and other sites are the minimum recommended for a reasonable viewing. Very often, however, time will be saved when you find a museum is closed (for example, early morning arrivals at Cherbourg will miss the Fort du Roule and save 30 minutes). Most museums are open (in the summer) from 9 a.m. until at least 6 p.m. (see pages 110/111). Out of the main tourist season many museums close despite their advertised hours.

No allowance is given for time for meals. If time is short, picnic breakfasts are recommended for ferry passengers arriving early in the morning, to be eaten somewhere along the tour, with a thermos each day for coffee. Picnic lunches may be purchased in any of the towns or villages on the route. A French long loaf (une baguette) with some slices of (tranches de) cheese (fromage) or ham (jambon) with some tomatoes (des tomates) and some apples (des pommes) might suffice.

Bon appétit et bon voyage!

TOUR MODULES

MODULES FOR BASIC TOURS
(all keep north of, or close to, the N13 Cherbourg/Caen road and are listed from west to east)

ADDITIONAL MODULES FOR FULL TOURS
(in historical sequence)

STE. MERE MODULE

Begins: 3m (5km) SW of Ste. Mère Eglise (on the N13 23m, 37km, south of Cherbourg).

Ends: In Ste. Mère Eglise.

Total distance: 7m (11km)) excluding

Estimated time (hr:min): Travel 0:35 + Visits 2:00 = Total 2:35) the link

Your tour will have brought you just west of Chef-du-Pont, parked by a memorial, facing the river Merderet.

Early in the morning of D-Day, aircraft carrying American paratroops of the 82nd Airborne Division flew from England across the Channel Islands and arrived over the area where you are now, two hours after midnight. The aim of the landing was to hold the western end of the allied invasion area to protect the forces landing by sea from German counter-attack until they were firmly established ashore. The weather was cloudy and there was much anti-aircraft gunfire ("flak"). As a result the pilots had difficulty in positioning themselves correctly for the drops and the troops landed over a wide area.

To your right and to your left they would have struggled to find each other in the dark before making their way to Ste. Mère Eglise which was captured at 4 a.m. They had a particular problem where you are now, for the area either side of the river Merderet just ahead of you had been flooded by the Germans. In certain seasons it floods naturally and you may be lucky to see it in that state. This will give you an awesome impression of the difficulties that would have been encountered by a fully equipped paratrooper landing in the water - in the dark. Sadly, many were drowned as they struggled to make for the higher ground.

Read the memorial, then take a closer look at the river by crossing the bridge ahead and immediately turning right. Turn right twice more to keep by the river, then go through **Gueutteville**, turning left at a small T-junction in the village. At the next T-junction where the only sign is on the left (back to "Gueutteville"), turn right onto a wider road. Just before you cross the river again, stop on the verge.

This is La Fière where a fierce battle took place as the Americans tried to reach the high ground ahead of you.

Drive on into **Ste. Mère**, turn right, drive to the far end of the square, turn left and park by the church.

If you are here in the tourist season, you will have no doubt already noticed the effigy of an American paratrooper hanging from his parachute caught on one of the

spires on the church roof. This commemorates the incident when the unfortunate soldier hung there for several hours feigning death to avoid being shot. He was eventually rescued and taken prisoner.

Visit the church to see the bullet holes on the pillar just inside the door and to admire the paratroopers' window on the far side. Then visit the **U.S. Airborne Museum** and the adjacent **C47 Museum** which houses one of the Dakota ("C47") transport aircraft used in the air-drop [2 hrs].

LINKS (refer to main tour page for time required to finish)

TOURS A, G, J, L: follow the UTAH - SOUTHBOUND MODULE (page 13).

TOUR B, E, H/FULL K : [If you have a spare two hours and wish to divert from the tour to follow the short COBRA MODULE, follow FULL F (below). The module is 1 hour and the return to Bayeux is 1 hour. Otherwise, read on.] Return to the main street and turn left, following signs to **Carentan** and **Caen**. As you reach **Bayeux,** turn right at the large roundabout (with the beflagged memorial to General de Gaulle in the middle) onto the D5a. After 0.75m (1.2km) you will see the war cemetery on your right and then the museum on your left. Park at the museum. **[36m, 58km: 0h 55m].** Now follow the BAYEUX MODULE (page 23).

TOURS C, I : Return to the main street and turn left, following signs to **Carentan** and **Caen**. After **Osmanville** (16m, 26km) there is a bend to the right and after 1m (2km) **La Cambe German cemetery** will be seen behind a wall on your right. Park in the lay-by. **[20m, 32km: 0h 35m].** Now follow the OMAHA - EASTBOUND MODULE (page 17).

TOUR D: Return to main tour (Basic D page 83, Full D page 84).

BASIC F, K: If you wish to follow the short COBRA MODULE (1 hour) follow FULL F (below) from now on. If not, return to main tour (Basic F page 88, Basic K page 100).

FULL F: Return to the main street and turn left, following signs to **Carentan**. Carry on for 2m (3km) and turn right onto the D174 towards **St. Lo**. Go through **St. Jean-de-Daye** and at **Pont-Hébert** turn right (signposted **St. Gilles**) onto the D92, then left onto the D77. When this reaches the D900 road, turn right (signposted **Périers**) and immediately park in the lay-by. **[25m, 40km: 0h 50m].** Now follow the COBRA MODULE (page 46).

UTAH - SOUTHBOUND MODULE

Begins: Ste. Mère Eglise (on the N13 23m, 37km, south of Cherbourg).
Ends: At D129/D329 junction near Hiesville (4m, 6km, SE of St Mère).

Total distance: 17m (28km)   ) excluding
Estimated time (hr:min): Travel 1:20 + Visits 0:40 = Total 2:00   ) the link

Your tour will have brought you to the town square at Ste. Mère Eglise.

You have heard about the American paratroops who landed in the early hours of D-Day to secure the western end of the invasion area and to capture this town. More paratroops were dropped south-east of here with a different task.

Utah Beach, one of the two landing beaches used by American forces on D-Day, is just six miles due east of here. Inland from the beach is a two-mile wide stretch of water-meadows and the only way across these is by a series of causeways. The task of these paratroops was to attack German positions on four of these causeways and secure them for the forces coming off the beach. We are now going to drive along the northernmost causeway.

Return to the main street and turn left, following signs to **Ecoquenéauville**. Go through this hamlet and after 0.8m (1.3km) turn left through **Turqueville** on the D129/D423 to **St. Martin**, where you turn left to **"La Mer"** (the sea). To your right, you will now have a good view of the causeway and the water-meadows. You will also shortly see the first of the roads named after U.S. soldiers killed in the area. At the D421 beach road, bear right to the **Leclerc Monument**, with French vehicles on display, which was raised in honour of the Free French troops who landed here some time later, led by the General of that name.

Continue along with the beach to your left, passing the next causeway (D67), and park when you reach **Utah Beach Museum**.

Walk onto the dunes and look down on the beach [10 mins].

As the fleet of landing craft and floating tanks approached at six in the morning, the navy started to fire on the German defences. At the same time over 1,000 allied bombers bombarded the shoreline, breaking off ten minutes before the first craft landed at 6.30. However, due to cloud, not all the targets were hit. This could have been serious, but the strong winds blew the invasion force somewhat south of their intended landfall towards a less fortified area.

The landing area extended from here to about two and a half miles to your left. As elsewhere, the beach was covered in spikes topped with explosives which could rip open the side of a landing craft - see the photograph on page 85. The dunes were mined and covered in barbed-wire entanglements. Once through the dunes, they had to cope with the water meadows, which the Germans had flooded. Headway was understandably slow, but by nightfall 23,000 men and 1,700 vehicles had landed.

Visit the memorials, the tank and the museum, if it is open [30 mins]. Note that the café is built on an old German battery.

We are now going to return to the N13 along another of the causeways. From the car park, take the D913 towards **Ste. Marie-du-Mont**.

On the way you will see on the left a statue commemorating 800 Danes who landed at Utah. Notice also the high church tower which was so helpful as a marker for the paratroops in the half-light of near-dawn.

Turn right at the church onto the D70 (**St. Mère**).

The most concentrated landings by paratroops of the U.S. 101st Airborne Division were in the fields to your left, although many were scattered over a wide area. Each man had been given a toy cricket that made a clicking noise to enable them to find each other in the darkness. Remarkably they came together in sufficient numbers to complete their task successfully.

Take the second left (D129 **Hiesville**) and stop at the junction of the second of two roads signed to that village, by the Pratt Memorial.

Read the memorial. Brigadier General Pratt and five others were killed just behind the memorial when over fifty gliders landed here just as dawn broke, with many crashing or hitting hedges. These troops had the task of supporting the paratroops who had landed earlier to secure the causeways.

LINKS (refer to main tour page for time required to finish)

TOURS A, G, J, L : Continue on (don't turn left to Hiesville), immediately forking right to follow signs to **Carentan** and **Caen**. In 13m (21km) you will reach **Osmanville** soon after which the road will bend to the right. After 1m (2km) **La Cambe German cemetery** will be seen behind a wall on your right. Park in the lay-by. **[16m, 26km: 0h 35m]**. Now follow the OMAHA - EASTBOUND MODULE (page 17).

UTAH - NORTHBOUND MODULE

Begins: At the D129/D329 junction near Hiesville (4m, 6km, SE of St. Mère Eglise).

Ends: 3m (5km) SW of Ste. Mère Eglise (on the N13 23m, 37km, south of Cherbourg).

Total distance: 20m (32km)   ) excluding
Estimated time (hr:min): Travel 1:25 + Visits 0:40 = Total 2:05   ) the link

Your tour will have brought you to the Pratt Memorial.

Read the memorial. Brigadier General Pratt and five others were killed just behind the memorial when over fifty gliders landed here just as dawn broke, with many crashing or hitting hedges. What had these troops come to do?

Utah Beach, just five miles north east of here, was the western end of the invasion area and was one of the two landing beaches used by the American forces on D-Day. Inland from the beach is a two-mile wide stretch of water meadows and the only way across these is by a series of causeways. Early in the morning of D-Day, paratroops of the 101st Airborne Division landed near here to attack German positions on four of these causeways and secure them for the forces coming off the beach. They were later relieved by the troops who landed in the gliders here.

Continue along the D129 and at the crossroads turn right onto the D70 towards **Ste. Marie-du-Mont.**

The most concentrated landings by the U.S. paratroops were in the fields to your right, although many were scattered over a wide area. Each man had been given a toy cricket that made a clicking noise to enable them to find each other in the darkness. Remarkably they came together in sufficient numbers to complete their task successfully. As you approach the village, notice the high church tower which was so helpful as a marker for the paratroops in the half-light of near-dawn.

Turn left in Ste. Marie-du-Mont towards **Utah Beach.**

The sections of road are here named in memory of U.S. soldiers killed in the area. On the way you will see on the right a statue commemorating 800 Danes who landed at Utah.

At Utah Beach, park in the car park.

As the fleet of landing craft and floating tanks approached at six in the morning, the navy started to fire on the German defences. At the same time over 1,000 allied bombers bombarded the shoreline, breaking off ten minutes before the first craft landed at 6.30. However, due to cloud, not all the targets were hit. This could have been serious, but the strong winds blew the invasion force somewhat south of their intended landfall towards a less fortified area.

Walk onto the dunes and look down on the beach [10 mins].

The landing area extended from here to about two and a half miles to your left. As elsewhere, the beach was covered in spikes topped with explosives which could rip open the side of a landing craft - see the photograph on page 85. The dunes were mined and covered in barbed-wire entanglements. Inland behind you the going was made difficult by the water-meadows which the Germans had flooded, leaving only the causeways for the troops and vehicles to cross. These were well covered by enemy positions, though they had been attacked earlier by the airborne troops. Headway was understandably slow, but by nightfall 23,000 men and 1,700 vehicles had landed.

Visit the memorials, the tank and the museum, if it is open [30 mins].   Note that the café is built on an old German battery.

From the car park, take the D421 coast road, signposted **Ravenoville**, (passing another of the causeways, the D67) as far as the **Leclerc Monument**, with French vehicles on display. It was raised in honour of the Free French troops who landed here some time later, led by the General of that name.

As the road bears left, turn inland onto the D423 to **St. Martin-de-Varreville.**

This is the northernmost causeway of the four used by the liberating forces.

Turn right in St. Martin and follow the D423/D129 to **Turqueville.**   There turn left at **"La Croix Pan"** then right for **Ecoquenéauville** and **Ste. Mère Eglise.**

In the main street, pass the square on your right (you'll be coming back later), then turn left signposted **Chef-du-Pont.**   Go under the N13, fork left on the D67 and, just after Chef-du-Pont (2.5m, 4km) as the river comes into view, park by the memorial on the right.

LINKS (refer to main tour page for time required to finish)

TOURS B, C, D, E, F, H, I, K : Follow the STE. MERE MODULE (page 11).

OMAHA - EASTBOUND MODULE

Begins: German war cemetery of La Cambe just west of the village of that name on the N13 14m (23km) west of Bayeux.

Ends: Longues-sur-Mer on the coast 5m (8km) north of Bayeux.

Total distance: 26m (42km)   ) excluding

Estimated time (hr:min): Travel 1:40 + Visits 2:40 = Total 4:20   ) the link

Your tour will have brought you to La Cambe cemetery, parked facing east.

LA CAMBE GERMAN WAR CEMETERY

If you have already visited a British or U.S. cemetery you will notice a strong contrast. The Germans are here buried three or more to a grave, with headstones lying flat on the ground [30mins].

[On the right of the cemetery there is a clean W.C. (H = Herrn = Hommes = Men : D = Damen = Dames = Women).]

POINTE-DU-HOC

From the cemetery continue towards **Bayeux,** but almost immediately turn left onto the D113, signposted **Grandcamp-Maisy.** Take the second right, signposted **Criqueville-en-Bessin.** Here turn left at the church. At the T-junction, turn right on the D514 coast road and in 1.3m (2km) turn left to the German fortified area known as **Pointe-du-Hoc** and park.

This was bombarded from the air and from the sea and was quickly taken by U.S. Rangers who scaled the cliffs. It has been preserved just as it was in 1944.

Read the board in the car park and visit the site [30 mins].

Continue along the coast road and at **Vierville-sur-Mer** (4m, 7km) turn left, signposted "**St Laurent par la cote**". Park in the National Guard Memorial car park ahead of you. This is the infamous Omaha beach. Read the memorial. [20mins].

On your left you will see (used as the base of a pier) part of the Mulberry floating harbour that was wrecked in a storm that came 13 days after D-Day. Other parts were taken to Arromanches to repair the Mulberry there. You will see this on the Gold Module.

OMAHA BEACH

Although the Germans were expecting an invasion somewhere and at some time, they thought it would probably be in the Calais region, due to the short sea crossing. The weather on D-Day was awful and an invasion was certainly not expected on that day. However, unfortunately for the Americans due to land at 6.30 a.m. on Omaha, the Germans happened to have chosen that night to hold an anti-invasion exercise on these very cliffs. Many landing craft, filled to the brim, in waves up to four feet high, hit sandbanks a little way off shore. Thinking they had reached the beach, troops jumped into the water and were dragged beneath the waves by the weight of their equipment. Murderous fire rained down from the cliff tops on those who made the beach. They had few places to hide amid wrecked landing craft, burning vehicles and exploding stores of ammunition. The strip of land between the beach and the cliffs was mined and strung with barbed wire and it is not surprising that there were over 3,000 casualties on that day in the area you can see ahead of you.

Boats were lowered twelve miles out in the rough seas - too far, some say. Ten landing craft were swamped, 23 guns were lost and only 3 of 16 bulldozers for clearing wreckage reached the shore. Of the 29 floating tanks launched four miles out, 27 sank.

In spite of these set-backs, with the help of eleven destroyers a half mile off shore, the Americans managed miraculously to obtain a foothold at the top of the cliffs. By midnight, 34,000 men had landed.

[Omaha - Westbound Module readers should now return to page 21]

Continue along the beach road until it starts to turn inland at a memorial.

You are now about to drive up one of only four exits from the beach for the tanks and other vehicles. They were heavily defended on the slopes on either side.

ST LAURENT U.S. WAR CEMETERY

Continue on to re-join the coast road. Turn left and just after the **Colleville** village-sign, turn left to the huge U.S. cemetery.

Compare the style with those of British and German cemeteries. You will notice the Jewish Stars of David haphazardly situated amongst the crosses. [1 hour].

PORT-EN-BESSIN

Return to the coast road and in 5m (8km) you will reach the port of **Port-en-Bessin** (see the photograph on page 20). If time is going well, spend a few minutes driving into this little town - there are several restaurants here.

It had been well defended by the Germans as they knew that the Allies would be desperate to obtain a harbour as soon as possible for the landing of supplies. In the event Royal Marine Commandos took the town at dawn on 8th June.

LONGUES BATTERY

Return to the coast road on the one way system following **Toutes Directions** and then turn left signposted **Arromanches** through **Commes** towards **Longues-sur-Mer** (3m, 5km). In Longues after passing the church standing alone on the right, turn left signposted **Batterie de Longues**. Park at the Battery car park.

There were four guns here which were capable of hitting the invasion fleet. In spite of accurate bombing, these strong concrete batteries were still in action as the ships approached. HMS Ajax brought its guns to bear and in twenty minutes three of the guns were silenced, two of them by shells that incredibly passed right through the slits!

Visit the battery. [20 mins].

Return to the D514 coast road.

LINKS (refer to main tour page for time required to finish)

TOURS A, J/BASIC C, I, L/FULL G: Carry straight over the D514 onto the D104 **Bayeux** road, forking right over the river just after Vaux-sur-Aure and going straight over the roundabout as you approach the Bayeux ring road. Turn right at the lights and at the roundabout (with the beflagged General de Gaulle memorial in the middle) turn left. After 0.75m (1.2km) you will see the war cemetery on your right and then the museum on your left. Park at the museum. **[6m, 10km: 0h 20m]**. Now follow the BAYEUX MODULE (page 23).

BASIC G/FULL C, I, L: Turn left along the D514 coast road to **Arromanches**. Follow signs to **Musée du Débarquement** and park near the museum. **[5m, 8km: 0h 15m]**. Now follow the GOLD - EASTBOUND MODULE (page 26).

OMAHA - WESTBOUND MODULE

Begins: Longues-sur-Mer on the coast 4m (6km) north of Bayeux.

Ends: German war cemetery of La Cambe just west of the village of that name on the N13 14m (23km) west of Bayeux.

Total distance: 26m (42km)) excluding

Estimated time (hr:min): Travel 1:40 + Visits 2:40 = Total 4:20) the link

Your tour will have brought you to the Battery car park at Longues-sur-Mer.

LONGUES BATTERY

There were four guns here which were capable of hitting the invasion fleet. In spite of accurate bombing, these strong concrete batteries were still in action as the ships approached. HMS Ajax brought its guns to bear and in twenty minutes three of the guns were silenced, two of them by shells that incredibly passed right through the slits!

Visit the battery. [20 mins].

Port-en-Bessin: General Bernard Montgomery talking to French fishermen [IWM]

PORT-EN-BESSIN

Return to the village, turn right and in 3m (5km), you will reach the port of **Port-en-Bessin** (see the photograph on page 20). If time is going well, spend a few minutes driving into this little town - there are several restaurants here.

It had been well defended by the Germans as they knew that the Allies would be desperate to obtain a harbour as soon as possible for the landing of supplies. In the event Royal Marine Commandos took the town at dawn on 8th June.

ST. LAURENT U.S. WAR CEMETERY

Return to the coast road on the one way system following **Toutes Directions** and then turn right signposted **Grandcamp Maisy.** Just after **Colville-sur-Mer** (4m, 7km) turn right to the huge U.S. cemetery.

Compare the style with that of a British war cemetery that you may have seen. You will notice the Jewish Stars of David haphazardly situated amongst the crosses. [1 hour].

OMAHA BEACH

Return to the coast road, continue on for 1m (2km) and at **St Laurent-sur-Mer** turn right down onto the beach road. The infamous Omaha beach is ahead and behind you. Park here for a moment and ponder the scene (or walk down onto the beach) reading the section headed "Omaha Beach" on page 18, then return to this page. [10 mins].

Drive to the far end of the beach road and park in the National Guard Memorial car park. Read the memorial. [10 mins].

On the beach you will see (used as the base of a pier) part of the floating harbour that was wrecked in a storm that came 13 days after D-Day. Other parts were taken to Arromanches to repair the Mulberry there.

You are now about to drive up one of only four exits from the beach for the tanks and other vehicles. They were heavily defended on the slopes on either side.

Continue up through **Vierville-sur-Mer** to the D514 coast road and turn right, signposted **Isigny.**

POINTE DU HOC

After 4m (7km) you will see a turning right to the German fortified area known as **Pointe-du-Hoc**. Turn in and park.

This was bombarded from the air and from the sea and was quickly taken by U.S. Rangers who scaled the cliffs. It has been preserved just as it was in 1944.

Read the board in the car park and visit the site. [30 mins].

LA CAMBE GERMAN WAR CEMETERY

Return to the coast road and turn right. Take the second left*, the D194 to **Cricqueville-en-Bessin**, where you turn right at the church (**Vers RN13**). At the D113 turn left, signposted **La Cambe**. At the N13, turn right, signposted **Carentan**. Very soon you will see La Cambe cemetery on your left behind a wall. Park on the right in the lay-by and visit the cemetery (take great care crossing the fast road).
You will notice a strong contrast with U.S. and British cemeteries. The Germans are here buried three or more to a grave, with headstones lying flat on the ground. [30 mins].
[On the right of the cemetery there is a clean W.C. (H = Herrn = Hommes = Men : D = Damen = Dames = Women).]

* If the causeway is flooded, carry on to Grandcamp Maisy, turn left onto the D199, then left onto the D113.

LINKS (refer to main tour page for time required to finish)

ONE DAY CIRCULAR TOUR FROM OUISTREHAM: You should now leave Basic Tour H. If you are on schedule it should be 5 p.m. Taking great care as the traffic moves very fast here, turn round and drive to **Bayeux**, around the ring road and on to the **Caen** ring road. Now follow the last paragraph on page 92 and thereafter. This will get you to Pegasus Bridge by 6 p.m. (the museum closes at 7 p.m. in season) and after a visit to Ranville you will reach Ouistreham by 8 p.m. in time for a leisurely meal before the late ferry.

TOURS B, D, E F, H, K: From the cemetery continue on the N13 to **Carentan** and **St. Côme-du-Mont** (13m, 21km). 2m (3km) after St Côme, turn right onto the D129, signposted **Hiesville**. At the first turning right (the D329 to Hiesville) stop on the verge just after the turning, staying on the D129. **[16m, 26km: 0h 35m].** Now follow the UTAH - NORTHBOUND MODULE (page 15).

BAYEUX MODULE

Begins and ends: Musée Mémorial on Bayeux ring road (with city visit options).

Total distance:	None (City glimpse 2m, 3km)	) excluding
Estimated time(hr:min):	Visits 2:00 (City glimpse: Travel 0:20)	) the link

Your tour will have brought you to the Musée Mémorial de la Bataille de Normandie on a boulevard named after Fabian Ware, who created the Commonwealth War Graves Commission.

The museum tells the story of the battle during the two months following D-Day, some of which is featured in the FULL tours in this booklet, leaving the events of D-Day itself to be told by the coastal museums.

British troops entered the outskirts of Bayeux on the evening of D-Day having met little resistance from the Germans. This was most fortunate for the city as its Gothic cathedral and medieval and Renaissance houses all survived the battle undamaged. The famous Bayeux Tapestry had been removed to a chateau near Le Mans for safekeeping. Tanks and infantry entered the centre of the city at noon the next day, 7th June, amid much rejoicing by the local inhabitants. This joy reached fever pitch when General de Gaulle, political leader of the Free French based in Britain, arrived a week later.

Visit this fine museum and its external exhibits. [1½ hours is allowed for this in your tour timing, to include the film, but many of you will stay longer!].

You may wish to visit the large war cemetery here - there are over 4,500 graves of a dozen nationalities, including German. Leave your car in the car park and walk to your right over the crossroads and cross to the other side of the ring road. On your way back to the car, cross the road (**very** carefully!) to the Memorial to the Missing, which remembers 1,800 men who fell in the Normandy campaign but have no known grave. The Latin inscription says "We, once conquered by William, have set free the conquerer's land". [30 mins].

The module and timing for your tour end here.

OPTIONAL

However, if you want to see something of this old city while you are here, you have two options, either to take a short drive to GLIMPSE the cathedral and old streets or to drive in, PARK, visit the cathedral, walk the old streets, maybe have a meal and possibly visit the Tapestry. Beware of many one-way streets.

TO GLIMPSE

Turn right out of the car park and, just after the cemetery, turn sharp right **(Rue de Verdun).** At the end of the straight, double back to the left **(Rue des Terres),** passing the tree-lined **Place Charles de Gaulle** on your right. The road becomes the **Rue Royale** and at the next crossroads turn right into **Rue St. Malo** which becomes **Rue St. Martin,** both of which have some old houses worth looking at. One of them (on a corner on the right) is the **Tourist Office.** Take the second right after that **(Rue Larcher)** past the **Post Office** (La Poste) and the **Town Hall,** and you will see the Gothic **cathedral** on your right. Continue straight on to return to the ring road.

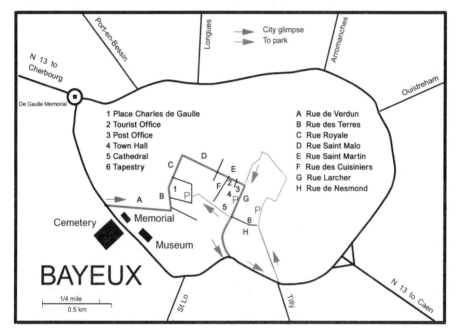

TO PARK

Follow "to glimpse" and try to park in front of the Town Hall. If parking looks difficult, continue straight on, passing the cathedral on your right, to the ring road. Turn left and left again, back into the town. Pass **Rue de Nesmond** on your left (the Tapestry is down there on the right) and you will see a car park on your left. If that is full, turn left when you can, to get back into the centre along **Rue Larcher** again. Now turn right, up by the side of the cathedral and you will come to **Place Charles de Gaulle** where there is further parking.

Visit the cathedral and see the plaque commemorating the liberators of Bayeux, the 56th Brigade. The Bayeux Tapestry (La Tapisserie de la Reine Mathilde) in the Rue de Nesmond will be of interest to some [1 hour]. It is in fact an embroidery, not a tapestry, and is 230 feet long by 20 ins high, telling the story of William the Conqueror's invasion of England in 1066. It was made for Bayeux cathedral in 1077 and there is an accompanying film explaining the historical background.

Return to the ring road along **Rue Larcher**.

LINKS (refer to main tour page for time required to finish).

BASIC A, C, I, J, L: At the ring road, turn left and carry on around for 2m (3km) then turn right onto the D516 to **Arromanches**. There follow signs to **Musée du Débarquement** and park near the museum. **[7m, 12km: 0h 20m].** Now follow the GOLD - EASTBOUND MODULE (page 26).

FULL A, B, C, D, E, G, H, I, J, K, L: At the ring road, turn left then almost immediately right (but keep in the left lane as you turn) onto the D6 south signposted **Tilly**. After 4m (7km) you will come to **Douet**. Stop just before the crossroads. **[5m, 8km: 0h 15m].** Now follow the TILLY MODULE (page 48).

TOUR F/BASIC D,K: Return to the ring road, turn right and carry on past the museum to the roundabout. Turn right onto the N13 and, at the third traffic lights, turn left onto the D104 (signposted **Longues** on the nearside of that road), straight over the small roundabout to **Longues-sur-Mer**, where you carry straight over to the **Batterie de Longues**. Park. **[6m, 9km: 0h 20m].** Follow the OMAHA - WESTBOUND MODULE (page 20).

BASIC B, E, G, H: Return to main tour (B page 78, E page 86, G page 90, H page 92).

GOLD - EASTBOUND MODULE

Begins: Arromanches (6m, 10km) north-east of Bayeux.
Ends:　　Ouistreham.

Total distance:	27m (43km)	) excluding
Estimated time (hr:min): Travel 2:35 + Visits 2:50 = Total 5:25		) the link

Your tour will have brought you near to the museum at Arromanches.

Arromanches lies just west of Gold Beach, the name given to one of the three beaches in the British sector between here and the port of Ouistreham twenty miles away. The others were Juno, where the Canadians landed, and Sword. All three are very similar being backed by sand dunes without the cliffs encountered by the Americans at Omaha, and only one small area of marshland (just east of here) - instead of the vast expanse of swamps to be found behind the other American beach at Utah.

This is not to say that the landings were easy, as you will read later.

MULBERRY HARBOUR

Arromanches itself is famous for the Mulberry harbour that was created here - the town has added "Port Winston" to its name in honour of Winston Churchill, who is said to have originated the idea. When you go into the museum you will see a clever model of Mulberry. The harbour consisted firstly of a three-mile semi-circle of huge concrete blocks, each five-storeys high, to create a harbour wall. They called them Phoenixes and all 146 of them, as with everything else, had to be towed across from England. Within this area floating piers led back to the shore (see the photograph on page 27).

It was a remarkable invention, but one that nearly died just as it was about to become useful. The components started to arrive the day after D-Day, struggling in the heavy seas. Within twelve days most of the Phoenixes were in place and the floating piers were half finished. The next day disaster struck.

A violent storm appeared from nowhere. Two and a half miles of floating roads being towed across the Channel were in sight of Arromanches when the raging seas swallowed them up. Over the following three days the winds blew and caused havoc not only here but at a second Mulberry being built at Omaha. The massive Phoenixes, unbelievably, were pushed around by the waves which rushed into the harbour and wrecked not only the piers, but many of the ships in the harbour.

When the gale subsided, the American Mulberry was a total wreck and was abandoned. Parts of it were used to repair the one here which was in more protected waters and was not so badly damaged. Nonetheless 800 craft had ended up on the beach.

The storm could have wrecked not only the Mulberries but the whole invasion, as the port was a vital link for ammunition, fuel, food and other stores to reach the fighting forces.

[Gold - Westbound Module readers should now return to page 39.]

A Mulberry harbour pontoon [© U.S. Army]

Visit the museum. It is quite small but worth an hour's visit including a good film. You may have to wait a while for the version in English so when you arrive ask when it is due to start. [1 hour].

Return to your car and make for the D514 signposted **Courseulles**. As you reach the top of the hill just east of Arromanches, stop and park near the tall column.

This area was heavily fortified and gave the Germans a magnificent view of the invasion fleet with superb opportunities to use their guns towards Gold beach to your right. Unfortunately for them, HMS Belfast (now a floating museum in the Port of London by Tower Bridge) had other ideas and its massive shells soon put paid to the Germans' plans.

Leave the car to look out a mile across the sea to the remains of the Mulberry.

Continue your drive eastwards and at the bottom of the hill, after the **Asnelles** village-sign, turn left at a telephone kiosk to the far end of the promenade. Park by the German gun emplacement and read the plaques on the wall.

GOLD BEACH

You are now at the beginning of Gold Beach and this is where the Royal Hampshire Regiment with tanks of the Essex Yeomanry landed at 7.25 a.m. on D-Day. The scene then was very different from today.

THE LANDINGS

The beaches were thick with steel spikes, topped with explosives, which could easily blow a hole in the bottom of a landing craft (see the photograph on page 85). The shore-line was heavily laced with barbed-wire and mined, with well-armed bunkers placed at intervals.

To combat these known threats, the British used not only conventional tanks but a series of armoured vehicles known as Hobart's Funnies, named after the general who developed them. They were mainly based on the hull of a tank and each had a special piece of equipment - a revolving drum on the front with chains attached that exploded mines ahead of the vehicle (the "flail" tank), a roll of matting that unravelled under the tank as it approached soft ground, a flame-thrower, a mortar with dustbin-sized bombs, bundles of wood for filling anti-tank ditches, or bridges for crossing wider gaps. Others were equipped as recovery vehicles to pull damaged vehicles off the road.

The Americans had been offered the use of these for Utah and Omaha and must surely have regretted their decision not to do so, for they enabled the British to make swifter headway across the beaches and shoreline than was achieved by the Americans, particularly at Omaha.

Immediately before the landings the shore batteries were bombarded by shells from a hundred ships and bombed by the RAF. Unfortunately, due to cloud, in an effort to avoid hitting the landing craft, many of the bombers dropped their loads a little late and they landed just behind the German bunkers. Thus, although the occupants were dazed from the intense attack, many of the batteries were still intact and were ready with a deadly welcome for the invading troops as they leapt from their landing craft.

Another invention for D-Day was floating tanks, known as D D tanks. This stood for duplex-drive as the engine drove two propellers as well as the wheels. With the help of a kind of rubber ring, they could be launched way out to sea and make their way ashore individually to give immediate support on arrival at the beach, instead of arriving all bunched together in a landing craft, with the possibility of them all sinking or being blown up together.

In the event, as the sea was very rough with waves of over four feet, several sank on the way in. Seeing this the rest wisely chose to stay on their landing craft.

The infantry embarked on their small landing craft from mother ships six miles offshore. The craft were lowered into the sea empty and the troops had to clamber down rope netting and jump at the right moment into the heaving boat. Many landed so heavily with all their attached equipment that they broke their legs. Others, sadly, fell between the ship and the landing craft and sank like stones. Their journey across to the shore was not ideal as a prelude to their forthcoming battle, as their little craft were tossed around by the wind and waves. Many, already sick with apprehension, were now physically sick as well - and all were soaked from spray.

In spite of all this, the landings at the three beaches were, in military terms, a success and by the end of the day forward elements had reached five to six miles inland.

[Gold Module - Westbound readers should now return to page 34].

Go onto the beach if you wish, then return to the car. [10 mins].

From the bunker turn left to the main road and turn left again. As you rise up the hill ahead, note the marshy ground to your left that had to be avoided by the invaders.

Just over the brow of the hill and immediately after the **Vers-sur-Mer** village sign, stop just before the small crossroads. Park off the road on the grass verge.

This was an area of heavy German fortification based around the Fleury battery, remains of which are becoming hidden in the housing estate up on your right. The land all around was mined and there were many gun emplacements on the slope to your right and slit trenches filled with mortars and machine guns. They were attacked by the Green Howards regiment who met probably one of the stiffest oppositions in this sector. It was here that the only VC of D-Day was won - by Company Sergeant Major Stan Hollis. In spite of heavy fire aimed right at him, he managed on two occasions to run towards the enemy position and kill its occupants, thus saving the lives of his own men.

If you look at the photograph on page 38 you will recognise the scene across the road. This was the Green Howards exit road.

JUNO BEACH

Drive through **Vers** and after 2 miles (3km), just before **Courseulles-sur-Mer**, at a traffic light, you will see a sign to the left to the **Juno Beach Memorial**. Turn here and park at the beach. [10 mins].

This is the beginning of the Canadian landing beach which only covered a small area as there are a number of rocks offshore to either side of the town. The Canadians were supported by the Royal Engineers and one of their Funnies, a Churchill tank with its dustbin mortar for blowing up enemy pillboxes, can be seen in front of you. There is also a Cross of Lorraine commemorating the Free French forces who assisted in the liberation of their homeland.

Walk onto the beach, then return to your car. Drive back to the main road and turn left into **Courseulles**. As you go over the second bridge (a swing one across the marina), turn left at the lights and when you see the **Sherman tank** on display, park on the left in front of the **Aquarium**. There are several restaurants here.
There is also a **WC** if you need one - walk down the road behind the Sherman, across the traffic lights and into the town hall car park on the left behind the railings. On the left is the WC (unisex) next to the entrance marked Police.
In any event, look at the Sherman tank and read the board. This was a DD tank that never made the shore and sank three miles out - it was recovered in 1970. There are a number of memorials around this open area and you may like to read the two on the right of the aquarium and see the other part of Juno beach there. [15 mins].

Further Canadian regiments landed east of here at Bernières, but as there is then a stretch of four miles before Sword Beach, we are now going inland.

From the Sherman take the road back the way you came in, but at the lights don't go right, across the marina, but carry straight over, following signs to **Caen**. At the roundabout with posts around it, turn left and after a third of a mile, take the first right, the D170 to **Reviers** (the signpost is on the right facing away from you). Stop on the verge after half a mile or so, just before a wood from where you might see a river.

This was the route taken by the Canadian Regina Rifles whose first task was to secure the bridge over the River Seulles to your right. They reached Reviers as early as 10.30 a.m. and by the next day had reached Bretteville on the N13 six miles south of here.

In Reviers turn right onto the D35 signposted Bayeux down the hill to the River Seulles. Having crossed the river, turn around in the road to your right.

You will see how much the river spreads and how important it was to keep the bridge intact.

Drive back to Reviers and park in the lay-by on the left in the centre of the village. At the parapet just before the lay-by, you will recognise the scene in the photograph on page 97.

Carry on along the D35 and after half a mile (1km) park at the **Canadian war cemetery.** Visit the cemetery where 2,000 Canadians are buried, including 335 who were killed on D-Day itself. Climb one of the watchtowers. There were German towers here on D-Day and you can see the view of Juno that they had from here. [20 mins].

Continue along the road across the D79 and stop just before the next crossroads.

This is the exit road from the beach at Bernières. The French Canadian regiment, Regiment de la Chaudière, came across here in front of you after clearing strong opposition from Germans dug in half-way down the road to your left. They reached Bény up to your right within four hours of landing and the French population were very surprised to hear their liberators speaking French instead of English.

Drive on and pause just before the next village.

Ahead is Tailleville which was a German head-quarters and thus strongly defended. It was not taken until 8 p.m. on D-Day. To your right is a wood beyond which are the remains of the Douvres radar station. The wood was occupied by a strong German force and, as they were on high ground, it was another eleven days before they were dislodged.

Drive on into **Tailleville**, turning right onto the D219 signposted **Basly** past the wood. As the wood ends, turn sharp left onto the **V3** towards **Douvres-la-Délivrande** and stop when you are under the first set of power lines.

This is the centre of the Douvres radar station. It was run by the German air force, the Luftwaffe, and covered the entire area between the two sections you can now see to your left and right. Occupied by 200 men it had radar towers, underground generators and tunnels connecting the various buildings and was defended by minefields and barbed wire. Being on high ground, it was difficult to attack but as the Germans had such a good view of the land ahead of you, which was the corridor between the Canadian and British armies, it had to be destroyed as soon as possible.

Several unsuccessful attacks were made and it was not until 17th June (D-Day + 11) did it succumb to a force of tanks and Royal Marine commandos, supported by flail tanks clearing the minefields as they came up the slope from Douvres.

If you wish to visit the remnants of the site to your left, park in the field entrance just before the next set of power lines. Walk along the edge of the fields. [15 mins].

Drive on down into Douvres, bearing left at the white fence, right at the T-junction (signposted **Froide Rue**), then immediately left signed **La Délivrande**. Fork right to **Douvres (Eglise)** and after the church turn left (no signpost) and go straight over the roundabout. At the main road, turn left then bear right signposted **Luc sur Mer**. At the lights, turn right and keep on the D35 through **Cresserons**. A half a mile after Cresserons (1km), you will see a small gas pumping station on the left of the road with wind pumps. Stop on the verge on your side just before you reach it.

The area you are now in was occupied throughout D-Day by the Germans and the crossroads ahead of you mark the beginning of the area held by British troops who had come off Sword Beach. They were being bombarded by German guns sitting on the ridge to your right. On your left is Lion-sur-Mer on the coast which was attacked by British Commandos, suffering heavy losses in the process. Late on D-Day German guns and infantry came across here where you are sitting, to attack the British forces. They took prisoners just off to your left but later decided to retreat back to the ridge and left the prisoners safe, well and free again - in a shell hole!

SWORD BEACH

Drive on. When the road bears sharp right, turn left signposted **Hermanville (Bourg)**. Fork left through the village and after half a mile (0.8km) you will see a well on the right opposite the church, next to the entrance to a war cemetery. Drive alongside and read the plaque. Bear right, signed **La Brèche**, over the D514, to a roundabout. Go straight across and park by the tank. This is one of Hobart's "Funnies". Walk onto the beach to the sea and look back, imagining what it would have looked like as you jumped off a landing craft on D-Day. [10 mins].

You are now not far from the eastern end of the whole invasion area and massive forces of tanks, commandos and infantry landed here from 7.25 a.m. One of the tasks of the commandos was to rush to Pegasus Bridge to support gliders and paratroops that had landed earlier in the morning (described in the Pegasus module). This was achieved. Less successful was the task of the others, which was to capture Caen. The strong wind created a high tide here, resulting in only thirty feet of beach being clear to receive the troops, artillery, tanks and stores that were constantly arriving. This caused dreadful congestion, delaying much of the forward movement that had been planned.

In spite of the shore line having received very heavy bombardment immediately before the invasion, the landing troops came under severe machine-gun fire as they jumped into the shallow water from their landing craft - made worse by the narrowness of the beach.

Return to your car. Turn left at the roundabout and join the D514. After the **Colleville-Montgomery** village sign, turn left at the lights. As you turn in to the road on the left, there is a memorial on your right which commemorates, in French, the first British graves of D-Day and the naming of the town after General Montgomery. The road then passes a bombed house kept as a memorial. Turn first right and continue on to the **No. 4 Commando Museum** (on your right). Park. The large building on the shore is the casino (Queen Normandy). *This was a German stronghold, but it was taken by French commandos who had landed with the British.* Visit the museum [30 mins].

Walk past the **Hotel Riva Bella** onto the beach memorial to view this end of Sword Beach, then return to the car.

LINK (refer to main tour page for time required to finish)

TOURS A, C, I, J, L/BASIC G: Carry on along the road signposted **Atlantic Wall Musée** and turn right at the T-junction past the Ouistreham ferry terminal, then follow signs firstly to **Autres Directions** and then to **Caen**. After 3m (5km) turn off onto the D514 **Bénouville** and **Ranville** (NOT the D35 Zone d'Activités de Bénouville) and keep straight on to **Pegasus Bridge**. Park just before the bridge. [5m, 7km: 0h 15m]. Now follow the PEGASUS MODULE (page 40).

GOLD - WESTBOUND MODULE

Begins: Ouistreham.
Ends: Arromanches (6m, 10km) north-east of Bayeux.

Total distance:	27m (43km)	) excluding
Estimated time (hr:min): Travel 2:35 + Visits 2:50 = Total 5:25		) the link

Your tour will have brought you to Ouistreham, opposite the No. 4 Commando Museum.

If it is wet, read the rest of this page (including "The Landings") in the car then walk to the beach memorial.

If it is dry walk past the **Hotel Riva Bella** (to the left of the Queen Normandy casino) onto the beach memorial and read on. [10 mins].

This is Sword Beach, the name given to one of the three beaches in the British sector between here and Arromanches twenty miles to the west. The others were Juno, where the Canadians landed, and Gold. All three are very similar being backed by sand dunes without the cliffs encountered by the Americans at Omaha, and only one small area of marshland (west of Courseulles) - instead of the vast expanse of swamps to be found behind the other American beach at Utah.

This is not to say that the landings were easy.

[Now read the section headed "The Landings" on page 28, then return to this page].

SWORD BEACH

You are now not far from the eastern end of the whole invasion area and massive forces of tanks, commandos and infantry landed here from 7.25 a.m. One of the tasks of the commandos was to rush to Pegasus Bridge to support gliders and paratroops that had landed earlier in the morning (described in the Pegasus module). This was achieved. Less successful was the task of the others, which was to capture Caen. The strong wind created a high tide here, resulting in only thirty feet of beach being clear to receive the troops, artillery, tanks and stores that were constantly arriving. This caused dreadful congestion, delaying much of the forward movement that had been planned.

The casino was a German stronghold, but it was taken by French commandos who had landed with the British.

Return to your car and visit the **No. 4 Commando Museum** if it is open. [30 mins].

Continue on the beach road until the town sign **Colleville-Montgomery**. Turn left here and stop just before the traffic lights. Here on the left is a memorial which commemorates, in French, the first British graves of D-Day and the naming of the town after General Montgomery. Turn right at the lights and after a mile fork right to a roundabout. Turn right here into the car park by one of Hobart's "Funnies". This is known as "La Brèche" and is the exact spot where many of the craft hit the beach. Walk onto the beach to the sea and look back, imagining what it would have looked like as you jumped off a landing craft on D-Day.

Return to the car and at the roundabout drive straight over to the main road and straight over again onto the D60b for **Hermanville-sur-Mer**. As you drive through the village you will see a well on your left opposite the church, next to the entrance to a war cemetery. Drive alongside and read the plaque.

Carry on through the village and turn right on the D35 signposted **Douvres**. After the third crossroads (signposted Lion-sur-Mer to the right) drive straight over till you reach a small gas pumping station on the right, with wind pumps. Stop on the verge just beyond it.

The area you are now in was occupied throughout D-Day by the Germans and the last crossroads mark the end of the area held by British troops who had come off Sword Beach. They were being bombarded by German guns sitting on the slope to your left. On your right is Lion-sur-Mer on the coast which was attacked from La Brèche by British Commandos, suffering heavy losses in the process. Late on D-Day German guns and infantry came across here where you are sitting to attack the British forces. They took prisoners just off to your right but later decided to retreat back to the slope and left the prisoners safe, well and free again - in a shell hole!

Drive on through **Cresserons** to **Douvres**. At the lights just before the twin-towered basilica turn left signposted **Caen**. Bear left with the road then immediately turn right signposted **Douvres (Eglise)** and **Anquerny**. At the church in Douvres-la-Délivrande, turn right signposted **Basly**, then at a T-junction turn right onto the D83 **(Basly)** and immediately left onto the D8 **(Basly)**. Just before the village end-sign, fork right at the white fence into a narrow lane. Stop under the first set of power lines.

JUNO BEACH

This is the centre of Douvres radar station, inland from Juno Beach. It was run by the German air force, the Luftwaffe, and covered the entire area between the two sections you can now see to your left and right. Occupied by 200 men it had radar towers, underground generators and tunnels connecting the various buildings and was defended by minefields and barbed wire. Being on high ground, it was difficult to attack but as the Germans had such a good view of the land behind you, which was the corridor between the Canadian and British armies, it had to be destroyed as soon as possible.

Several unsuccessful attacks were made and it was not until 17th June did it succumb to a force of tanks and Royal Marine commandos, supported by flail tanks clearing the minefields as they came up the slope from Douvres.

If you wish to, walk along the edge of the fields to your right to the remnants of the site [15 mins]. Return to your car.

The woods ahead to your half-right were occupied by a strong German force and, as they were on high ground, it was eleven days after D-Day before they were dislodged. Beyond the wood to your right is Tailleville which was a German headquarters and thus strongly defended. It overlooked the eastern end of Juno beach where the Canadians landed and, although the Canadians by-passed it at mid-day, it was not taken until 8 p.m. on D-Day.

Drive on, turning right through the wood and on to **Tailleville**, where you turn left onto the **Reviers** road (D35). Stop off the road at the power lines when you can see Bernières on the coast to your right.

The road running across you shortly is the exit road from the beach at Bernières. The French Canadian regiment, Regiment de la Chaudière, came across here in front of you after clearing strong opposition from Germans dug in half-way down the road to the right. They reached Bény up to your left within four hours of landing and the French population were very surprised to hear their liberators speaking French instead of English.

Cross over the Canadians' exit road and over the D79 and park at the **Canadian war cemetery.** Visit the cemetery where 2,000 Canadians are buried, including 335 who were killed on D-Day itself. Climb one of the watchtowers. There were German towers here on D-Day and you can see the view of Juno that they had from here. [20 mins].

Return to the car. *The next town is Reviers which was captured as early as 10.30 on D-Day morning by the Canadian Regina Rifles. Their first task was to secure the bridge across the River Seulles which you will see beyond the village.*

Leave the cemetery and drop down into **Reviers**. Go straight through the village on the D35, over the River Seulles and turn around in the road to your right.

You will see how much the river spreads itself here and how important it was to keep the bridge intact.

Drive back into Reviers and park in the lay-by on the left in the centre of the village. At the parapet just before the lay-by, you will recognise the scene in the photograph on page 97.   Carry on and immediately turn left onto the D170, later crossing straight over the D79 for **Courseulles**.   In Courseulles keep driving straight through the town.

If you need a **WC** at this point there is a unisex one on your right behind some railings just before a set of traffic lights.   It is the car park of the Town Hall and the WC is on the left next to the entrance marked Police.

Drive on until you reach the **Sherman tank** on display and park in front of the **Aquarium** [15 mins].   There are several restaurants here.   Look at the Sherman and read the board.   This was a DD tank that never made the shore and sank three miles out - it was recovered in 1970.   There are a number of memorials around this open area and you may like to read the two on the right of the aquarium and see the part of Juno Beach on which the Regina Rifles landed.

From the Sherman drive west (i.e. with the sea to your right), crossing over the yacht basin bridge, signposted **Vers-sur-Mer** and **Graye**.   In just over half a mile there is a signpost to **Juno Beach Memorial**.   Turn right here and park at the beach [10 mins].

This is the western end of the Canadian landing beach which only covered a small area as there are a number of rocks offshore to either side of the town.   The Canadians were supported by the Royal Engineers and one of their Funnies, a Churchill tank with its dustbin mortar for blowing up enemy pillboxes, can be seen in front of you.   There is also a Cross of Lorraine commemorating the Free French forces who assisted in the liberation of their homeland.

Walk onto the beach, then return to your car.   Drive back to the main road and turn right, through **Vers-sur-Mer**.   Just after the main road forks left, the ground starts to rise up.   Before you reach the village end-sign, there is a small crossroads. Stop immediately after the turning and park on the grass verge.

GOLD BEACH

This was an area of heavy German fortification based around the Fleury battery, remains of which are becoming hidden in the housing estate up on your left. The land all around was mined and there were many gun emplacements on the slope to your left with slit trenches filled with mortars and machine guns.   These were attacked by the Green Howards regiment who met probably one of the stiffest oppositions in this sector.   It was here that the only VC of D-Day was won - by

Company Sergeant Major Stan Hollis. In spite of heavy fire aimed right at him, he managed on two occasions to run towards the enemy position and kill its occupants, thus saving the lives of his own men.

If you look at the photograph below you will recognise the scene in front of you. This was the Green Howards exit road.

The Green Howards move inland from Gold Beach [IWM]

Continue on towards **Asnelles** noting what good defensive positions the machine guns had on the slope to your left. Turn right just after the Asnelles village sign, before the petrol station. Park by the German gun emplacement and read the plaques on the walls [10 mins].

This is the western end of Gold Beach where the Royal Hampshire Regiment with tanks of the Essex Yeomanry landed at 7.25 a.m. on D-Day. Many remains of the floating harbour can be seen in the sea - you will read about this shortly.

Go onto the beach if you wish, then return to the car.

Carry on along the promenade and re-join the D514, turning right for Arromanches, but at the top of the hill, park near the tall column overlooking the town.

This area was heavily fortified and gave the Germans a magnificent view of the invasion fleet with superb opportunities to use their guns towards Gold beach to your right. Unfortunately for them, HMS Belfast (now a museum in the Port of London by Tower Bridge) had other ideas and its massive shells soon put paid to the Germans' plans.

[Now read the section marked "Mulberry Harbour" on page 26, then return to this page].

Leave the car to look out a mile across the sea to the remains of the Mulberry.

Continue on down the hill into **Arromanches**, follow signs to **Musée du Débarquement** and park near the museum [1 hour].

Visit the museum. It is quite small but worth an hour's visit including a good film. You may have to wait a while for the version in English so when you arrive ask when it is due to start.

LINKS (refer to main tour page for time required to finish)

TOUR D/BASIC F, K: Take the D514 becoming the D516 to **Bayeux** where you turn **right** at the N13 ring road, signposted **Cherbourg**. At the roundabout (with the beflagged General de Gaulle memorial in the centre), turn left signposted **Caen** onto the D5a. After 0.75m (1.2km) you will see the war cemetery on your right and then the museum on your left. Park at the museum. **[7m, 12km: 0h 20m].** Now follow the BAYEUX MODULE (page 23).

TOUR B, E, H/FULL K: Continue along the D514 coast road, signposted **Port-en-Bessin**, to **Longues-sur-Mer** where you turn right signposted to **Batteries de Longues**. Park by the gun emplacements. **[5m, 8km: 0h 15m].** Now follow the OMAHA - WESTBOUND MODULE (page 20).

FULL F: Take the D514 becoming the D516 to **Bayeux** where you turn **left** at the N13 ring road. At the roundabout, take the road signposted **St. Lo** and at the next junction turn left on the D6 signposted **Tilly**. After 4m (7km) you will come to **Douet**. Stop just by the verge immediately before the crossroads. **[11m, 18km: 0h 25m].** Now follow the TILLY MODULE (page 48).

FULL G: Return to main tour (page 91).

PEGASUS MODULE

Begins: Pegasus Bridge at Bénouville midway (4m, 7km) between Caen and the ferry terminal at Ouistreham.

Ends: Ranville 1m (2km) east of Pegasus.

Total distance: 2m (3km)) excluding
Estimated time (hr:min): Travel 0:20 + Visits 1:20 = Total 1:40) the link

Your tour will have brought you to Pegasus Bridge named after the flying horse emblem of the Airborne Forces who were the first Allied troops to land in France on D-Day*.

The bridge crosses the canal from Caen to the sea and it was vital that Pegasus (and the next one you will cross, over the River Orne) should remain intact as the front line facing the Germans to the east was to be on the ridge ahead of you - the bridges would be the only means for supplies and reinforcements to cross those waterways. On the right just before the bridge is the famous café owned by the Gondrée family who were the first French people to be liberated. Each year on the anniversary of D-Day, they entertain veterans from the Airborne Forces.

* The original bridge is under threat for replacement to allow larger ships to pass this point. At the time of writing it is not known when this will take place or where the old bridge will be displayed.

Pegasus Bridge: British soldiers pass the spot where Lt. Brotheridge was shot [IWM]

To the right of the café is an excellent small museum. The manager speaks English and will give you a superb short explanation of the landings at Pegasus Bridge, complete with model and a short video film (for opening times, see Musée des Troupes Aéroportées on page 111). [45 mins].

Walk over the bridge and enter the path leading off diagonally to your right across the swamp [15 mins].
There you will see three plaques marking the spots where three gliders landed to capture the bridge before the Germans could blow it up. To achieve this the leading glider was instructed to land fifty yards from the bridge at 12.15 a.m. It did so exactly - but a minute late! All this was achieved in cloud, under constant anti-aircraft fire from the ground. As you cross the bridge you will pass the spot where the first Allied soldier to die on D-Day, Lt. Den Brotheridge, fell in the road (just opposite the café) as he raced across.

Continue along the road and stop just before the next bridge (across the River Orne). On your left is the area where two more gliders (another got lost) landed to capture it - see the plaque by the bridge.

Bear right onto the D37 towards **Ranville**, turning first right then immediately left to the church. Turn left and drive around the church wall to the British war cemetery. Park outside the cemetery [20 mins].
This is a small and very typical British war cemetery. Spend ten minutes walking around and reading the inscriptions. All died locally. The inscriptions at the bottom of each are chosen by the family of the deceased and some are very moving. One such, for a mere 19 year-old, reads "Maybe one day we shall understand".

Go into the churchyard through the hole in the wall and turn right to the main gate. Walk along the path to the left inside the wall.
These soldiers were buried here before the war cemetery was created. Near the end of the line is the gravestone of Lt. Brotheridge. Next to it is a plaque from the Gondrée family at the café, as "the 1st family to be liberated" remembering "the 1st soldier to fall".

Return to your car and carry on to the T-junction. You will see ahead of you the chateau that was used as the headquarters of General "Gusty" Gale, commander of the paratroops in this part of the campaign. Turn left and, at the crossroads:-

BASIC TOURS - turn left and immediately stop off the road.

FULL TOURS - go straight over onto the D223 **Bréville** road and stop by the side of the road after the wall, when you can see the fields to left and right.

LINKS (refer to main tour page for time required to finish).

FULL A to L: Now follow the MERVILLE MODULE (page 43).

BASIC A to L: *Half-an-hour after the glider landings at Pegasus Bridge, paratroops landed in the field behind the houses to your right, supported three hours later at 3.30 in the morning, by gliders. Their task was to clear the enemy out of Ranville. Due to bad visibility many gliders landed across the paths of others and many deaths and injuries were caused without the hand of the Germans.*

Drive straight on (with Ranville to your left) over **Pegasus Bridge** and over the crossroads (1m, 2km) then:-

[BASIC G, J, K: Before following your link below, you may wish to visit Caen museum and/or city (part of the Full Tour only - it is NOT included in your timing). To do so, continue over the bridge for **Caen** and at the ring road turn right signposted **Cherbourg** then after 2m (3km) turn off at the sign for **Mémorial** (the name of the museum). Then follow further signs to **Mémorial** and park in the car park. **[10m, 16km: 0h 25m]**. Now follow the CAEN MODULE (page 53).]

BASIC A, C, E, H, I, J, L: Return to main tour (A page 75, C page 80, E page 86, H page 92, I page 94, J page 98, L page 102).

BASIC B, D, F, K: Bear right to **Ouistreham**. At the ferry terminal keep to the left lane, following signs to the **Plage** (beach).
As the road bears left you will see in a side street a huge concrete tower built by the Germans to control the anti-aircraft defences of the port. Known as the flak tower, it now houses a museum.
Carry on until you reach a large building on the right, called **Queen Normandy**. This is the casino and on your left is the **No. 4 Commando Museum**. Park on the right, opposite the museum. **[6m, 9km: 0h 25m]**. Now follow the GOLD - WESTBOUND MODULE (page 34).

BASIC G: Continue over the bridge to **Caen** and at the ring road turn right signposted **Cherbourg** for the N13 to **Bayeux**. At the Bayeux ring road, turn left at the roundabout signposted **St. Lo**. Continue on the ring road for 1.25m (2km) and you will see the museum on your right. Park. **[26m, 42km: 0h 50m]**. Now follow the BAYEUX MODULE (page 23).

MERVILLE MODULE

Begins: Ranville just east of Pegasus Bridge 4m (6km) south of the ferry terminal at Ouistreham.

Ends: At the junction of the D513/D37b 1.2m (2km) east of Hérouvillette.

Total distance: 14m (23km)) excluding

Estimate time (hr:min): Travel 1:20 + Visits 0:20 = Total 1:40) the link

Your tour will have brought you just east of Ranville on the D223 between open fields.

Half-an-hour after the glider landings at Pegasus Bridge, paratroops landed in the field to your left, supported three hours later, at 3.30 in the morning, by gliders. Their task was to clear the enemy out of Ranville. Due to bad visibility many gliders landed across the paths of others and many deaths and injuries were caused without the hand of the Germans. On D-Day evening further gliders had to land on your right as the fields on the left were filled with the debris of the morning landings.

Continue up the road to **Bréville** on the ridge and, just before the crossroads, park on the left side of the road. Walk up onto the bank and look back across to Ranville, the River Orne and the canal.

You will see how vital it was that this ridge was captured to prevent the Germans from holding a perfect position for viewing, and firing on, the British front line. For this was to be the eastern edge of the Normandy invasion area to be held until August when the Americans planned (and did) work their way from the Cherbourg peninsula to a position due south of here, ready for the joint advance towards Germany.

Walk up to the crossroads and read the memorial. Return to the car. Turn right and, at the water towers, you will see the **Chateau St. Côme** on the left. Stop and read the memorial at the driveway entrance.

Bréville was very heavily defended and some bitter battles took place there. The Black Watch launched their attack on the village from here on 11th June but had to pull back. The next day men from Yorkshire and Devon tried again from the opposite direction and Bréville was taken - but 162 men were dead. Fighting was so intense and confused at the crossroads, that many of the British soldiers who died were killed by their own artillery support.

Turn around, go back over the crossroads to **Amfréville** and stop just before the tall trees by a memorial to No. 6 Commando in front of a huge barn. Each June since 1944 the owner of the farm has entertained his liberators here.

Fork right and carry on to **Sallenelles** - on the way look over to your left at Ouistreham at the beginning of Sword Beach. Turn right onto the D514 signposted **Deauville** and after 2m (3km), turn right at the lights, following signs to the **Batteries de Merville**.

Park in the battery car park and read the dramatic story on the notice boards, remembering that Sword Beach is just three miles to your right as you face the batteries. If you can get in, wander around and climb onto the battery "casemates". The tiny museum (in a casemate) may also be open. [20 mins].

Turn right out of the battery and at **Descanneville** turn right onto the D223. Take the second turning left onto the D95a through **Gonneville-en-Auge** and a few yards after the church carry straight on - don't bear right with the road. After 0.25m (0.4km), stop on the verge after the wall when you can see clearly to the left.

It was here that British paratroops landed to attack the Merville battery. The Germans had totally flooded the area just beyond from the waters of the River Dives and its tributaries. Many paratroops were drowned when their transport aircraft dropped them too far east, their heavy packs dragging them down in the dark of night.

In the same area Canadian paratroops landed to head for Varaville (to your half-left). They had the task of blowing up several bridges to prevent German reinforcements from reaching the ridge and Pegasus Bridge beyond.

At the main road turn left and then fork right onto the D27 signposted **A13**. **Immediately** the houses end you will cross the small bridge over the Divette that was blown up by the Canadians. Drive on a little way to see the network of ditches that the Germans flooded.

[If you are on FULL E and in a hurry to return to the EAST, this is the point to leave the tour - see "To return eastwards after Full E" on page 106.]

Turn around in the next driveway and return to **Varaville**, turning left onto the D513 signposted **Caen**. After 3m (5km), just after a left turn signposted **Bavent** and **Dozulé** (D224), stop in a lay-by on the right just after a house next to an open field.

You are now back on the ridge and the Chateau St Côme visited earlier is in the woods up to your right. The crossroads ahead was the rendezvous for the Canadians after they had blown the bridges.

LINKS (refer to main tour page for time required to finish)

FULL A, C, I: Continue over the crossroads to **Hérouvillette** and at the end of the village turn left (slightly hidden) onto the D37 to **Escoville**. In the centre, turn right (also slightly hidden) signposted **Touffréville/Sannerville** but stop as soon as you leave Escoville and park on the verge in the avenue of trees. **[2.5m, 4km: 0h 10m].** Now follow the GOODWOOD - SOUTHBOUND MODULE (page 61).

FULL B, D, E, F, G, K: Continue over the crossroads then immediately fork right onto the D244 for **Ranville** and **Bénouville**. Go over Pegasus Bridge and follow signs to **Ouistreham**. At the ferry terminal keep to the left, following signs to **Plage** (beach).
As the road bears left you will see in a side street on the left a huge concrete tower built by the Germans to control the anti-aircraft defences of the port. Known as the flak tower, it now houses a museum.
Carry on until you reach a large building on the right, called **Queen Normandy**. This is the casino and on your left is the **No. 4 Commando Museum**. Park on the right, opposite the museum. **[8m 13km: 0h 30m].** Now follow the GOLD - WESTBOUND MODULE (page 34).

FULL H, J: Return to main tour (H page 93, J page 99).

FULL L: Continue over the crossroads and carry straight along the D513 towards **Caen**. Just before the viaduct, keep in the left lane to turn left onto the ring road signposted **Cherbourg**. Continue to **Bayeux**. When the N13 arrives at the Bayeux ring road, turn left at the roundabout, signposted **St. Lo**. Continue on the ring road for 1.25m (2km) and you will see the museum on your right. Park. **[27m, 43km: 0h 45m].** Now follow the BAYEUX MODULE (page 23).

COBRA MODULE

Begins: At the D900/D77 crossroads just NW of Hébécrevon 3m (5km) west of St Lo.

Ends: At the D77/D149 crossroads just SW of Hébécrevon.

Total distance: 10m (16km)) excluding

Estimated time (hr:min): Travel 0:30 + Visits 0:15 = Total 0:45) the link

Your tour will have brought you to the junction of the D900/D77, parked in a lay-by on the D900, facing west (towards Périers).

This is the deadly bocage country, where the landscape consists of small fields bounded by high earth banks that are thick with the roots of the hedges on top. Lanes are deeply sunk, winding and narrow. It is a defender's paradise where the German tanks just sat, with only the tops of their turrets showing, awaiting the Americans as they struggled through this inhospitable countryside, knowing that every field could be their last.

An American infantry patrol in the bocage [© U.S. Army]

After the D-Day landings at Utah and Omaha beaches, the Americans crossed to the west coast of the Cotentin peninsula and made for Cherbourg which was liberated on 30th June. In the meantime, they held the line to their south, roughly due west from Carentan (11m, 18km, north of here). They then fought their way south until they were forced to a halt on a line just north of the road you are now on, from St Lo (behind you) to Périers. St Lo was captured on 19th July, but not before nearly every building had been destroyed.

The road ahead of you for the next 4m (7km) was the start line for Operation COBRA, the plan for the massive breakout southwards towards Avranches. It was achieved in six days - but not without tragedy. The area to your left was held by 40 tanks of a crack German Panzer division until they were all wiped out by a carpet of bombs dropped by 2,000 heavy bombers of the U.S. Air Force. Unfortunately 100 Americans were killed (including a General) when some of the bombs fell short, to the right of your road. The Americans then advanced from your right to the left making for Coutances and Avranches. During the bombing and the subsequent attack, 6,000 Germans met their end. You will shortly see this graphically illustrated in their cemetery.

Drive three miles (5km) along the start-line, then turn left onto the D29 signposted **Marigny.** After 2.6m (4km) turn left signed **Deutscher Soldatenfriedhof** (German war cemetery) and park when you get there. Glimpse at, or visit, the cemetery (you will see another on the Omaha Module) and read the display in the room on the left of the entrance. [15 mins].

Carry on, turning left at the T-junction to **La Chapelle-en-Juger.** *This village was flattened by the bombing that preceded Operation Cobra.* Turn right onto the D149 (**St. Lo**) and stop at the crossroads with the D77.

LINKS (refer to main tour page for time required to finish)

TOURS C, I: Turn left at the crossroads and follow signs to **Pont-Hébert** where you turn left on the N174 signposted **Cherbourg.** At the N13, turn left through **Carentan** and just after **St. Côme-du-Mont,** turn right onto the D219, signposted **Hiesville.** At the first turning right (the D329 to Hiesville) park on the verge just after the turning (staying on the D219). **[22m, 35km : 0h 55m].** Now follow the UTAH -NORTHBOUND MODULE (page 15).

FULL B, E, H, K: Turn right at the crossroads (no signpost) to **Gilles.** Turn left onto the D972 towards **St. Lo** (signposted on the left of the D972 as you turn) and follow signs to **Bayeux.** On reaching the ring road, turn left and you will shortly see the museum on your right. Park in the car park. **[31m, 50km: 1h 5m].** Now follow the BAYEUX MODULE (page 23).

TOUR F/BASIC K: All now follow Full Tour F (page 89).

TILLY MODULE

Begins: Le Douet on the D6 5m (8km) south of Bayeux.
Ends: Fontenay-le-Pesnel 2.5m (4km) east of Tilly.

Total distance:	14m (22km)	) excluding
Estimated time (hr:min):	Travel 0:45 + Visits 0:10 = Total 0:55	) the link

Your tour will have brought you just before the crossroads at Le Douet.

By 8th June, 2 days after D-Day, British tanks had reached as far south as this village 10 miles from the sea. Here they were met by the most powerful German tank division in the whole of Normandy - huge Tiger tanks, supported by anti-tank guns that could fire accurately over 3/4 mile and the much-feared multi-barrelled "Nebelwerfer" mortars. The British halted and called for air support but when the fighter-bombers came they unfortunately strafed their own side as well as the Germans. It was decided to move around the defending forces to the west so tanks set off down the road turning off to your right.

[Before turning right you may like to pay a short visit to the smallest war cemetery in Normandy, called Jerusalem, after the name of a nearby hamlet. There are 48 graves here. It is at the bottom of the incline 300 metres ahead of you on the left hand side. You can park on the right of the driveway that leads to the huge barn behind the cemetery. Visit the cemetery and return to the crossroads. [10 mins].

Turn right (or left if you've been to Jerusalem) signposted **Juaye-Mondaye**. Follow this road (D33) to **Bernières**, bear left signposted **Villers Bocage** and, at the end of Bernières, stop off the road after a bend to the right, just before a ruined stone barn when you can see the land away to the left and right.

As the tanks came through the village as you just did, they saw German Panther tanks at the crossroads behind you and succeeded in knocking them out.

To your right the 1st Hampshire Regiment saw very heavy fighting for the next week, making no progress against the Germans firmly hidden on the slope on your left.

Carry on to **Le Sanaudière**. This little hamlet was wiped out by heavy bombing during this period. Turn left onto the D13 (signposted **Tilly**). When you reach **Lingèvres**, park on the left just beyond the church. Stand by the road at the end of the church and compare the scene with the photograph on page 109. Carry on for a mile and a half (3km) and you will reach a war cemetery on the right at a crossroads. Park in front of the entrance (as close as you can, as its a fast narrow road).

The road you have just driven along, as far as Tilly (3/4 mile ahead of you) and beyond, was the German front-line for two weeks. During this time, they lost over 5,000 men (killed, wounded or captured) and over 120 tanks - but gave no ground. Many of these losses were caused by naval gunfire from 15 miles away in the Channel and by Typhoon aircraft. Tilly was totally destroyed.

Visit the cemetery if you wish [not included in the timing].

Turn right immediately after the cemetery and at the next junction turn right. Stop by the road.

The 2nd Devonshire Regiment reached here on 19th June and stayed for three weeks attempting to oust a powerful German tank regiment from Hottot-les-Bagues on the hill to your left.

Drive on along the winding road for over a mile (1.9km), then take the first turning left (no signpost) stopping as soon as you see the village in the distance.

From your left, the Devons made a strong attack on 11th July and, after a week's bitter fighting, the Germans, who were determined to hold the village, eventually withdrew.

Drive into the village, then turn left (no signpost) onto the D9, passing the Hottot War Cemetery to reach **Fontenay-le-Pesnel**. Go through the town and, soon after the town-end sign, park in the lay-by just after the beginning of the avenue of trees.

LINKS (refer to main tour page for time required to finish)

FULL TOURS A to L: Now follow the EPSOM MODULE (page 50).

EPSOM MODULE

Begins: Fontenay-le-Pesnel 3m (5km) east of Tilly.
Ends: Hill 112 at the D8/D36 junction 2.5m (4km) east of Evrecy.

Total distance: 14m (22km)   ) excluding
Estimated time(hr:min):   Travel 1:10 + Visits 0:00 = Total 1:10   ) the link

Your tour will have brought you just east of Fontenay-le-Pesnel, parked in the lay-by just after the beginning of the avenue of trees.

OPERATION EPSOM

Three weeks after D-Day Caen was still in German hands and Operation EPSOM was devised as part of a plan to encircle the town and establish a tank force on the Caen/Falaise road to the south.   The objective was to get there from the N13 Bayeux road west of Caen, down across the rivers Odon and Orne.

On the afternoon of 25th June, 6,000 men, 600 tanks and 300 guns, supported by three cruisers offshore, stood poised a mile and a half to your left and parallel with your road, ready to advance on Cheux and other villages to your half-right.   Early next morning heavy rain and mist hampered their progress and also grounded the planes that were not only going to provide fighter support but also to bomb Cheux as the tanks approached.   As the troops crossed your road and entered the sodden fields, they encountered mines and barbed-wire entanglements which, with the mortar and machine gun fire being directed at them from Cheux and from Rauray (on the hill to your right), caused many casualties.   As men died in the cornfields, their positions were marked by rifles stuck into the ground by their bayonets, with a helmet on top so that they could be found and buried later.

Drive on and take the first turning right (opposite the huge Coop Can building) to **Cheux,** where you turn right in the village.   Turn left at the village washhouse onto the D89 towards **Tourville.**   Stop on the bridge crossing over the N175.

Cheux had been battered to pieces by artillery and by the ships at sea and the Scottish infantry managed to reach this bridge by the afternoon (the N175 was then a railway).
The next day they tried to reach the River Odon a mile and a half ahead of you, taking the route you are about to drive.

Continue over the bridge, follow the road into **Tourville-sur-Odon,** go over the crossroads signposted **Esquay** and after a third of a mile (0.5km) stop at the monument on your right.   Read the plaque on the left face.

The Highlanders had taken the route on the run and as they came out of orchards further on below you into open cornfields, they were met by heavy machine-gun fire. They managed to cross the bridge with few additional casualties and set up a defensive circle 200 yards beyond the bridge. By the evening the tanks, held up in seas of mud caused by the torrential rain, caught up with them and secured the position.

Drive down to the bridge and pause on the grass just beyond it.

The next day (28th June) parties of Scotsmen moved along both river banks to your right to the next bridge a mile up river at Gavrus, to which this tour now takes you.

Drive on up the hill and turn around in the farm entrance on the left. Return over the bridge to Tourville and turn left onto the D675. Turn left at the main road (still called the D675, signposted Noyers Bocage) then very shortly left again, onto the D139 towards **Gavrus**. Cross over the first bridge and park on the verge before you reach the second.

When the Scots reached the two bridges, surprisingly they found them undefended. The rest of the battalion joined them down the road you have just come and a headquarters was established in a quarry behind you. Defences were set up beyond the next bridge and in the meadows on either side of you, awaiting tank support. Before the tanks arrived a fierce counter-attack from German infantry appeared from the right of Gavrus (up in the trees ahead) and the Scotsmen were forced to retreat to the two bridges and dig in. In the afternoon of the following day, fresh troops arrived and a firm line was held along the River Odon.

Whilst the final objective of the River Orne had not been reached, Operation EPSOM had made good headway and the 2,500 Scottish casualties had not been suffered in vain.

HILL 112
Drive on through **Gavrus** to **Evrecy**, turning left in the town onto the D8. Continue on through **Esquay** and park in front of a large monument on the right to the Wessex Division.

On your right is an area known as Hill 112 (being a height of 112 metres). From the wood there, German Tiger tanks caused in all a total of 7,000 casualties. It was first taken by British tanks on 29th June (while the Scots were at Gavrus), but they were driven back next day. A further attempt on 10th July caused the death of 800 men of the Duke of Cornwall regiment.
Gavrus, Evrecy and Hill 112 were finally captured on 12th August, six weeks after EPSOM.

Drive on and park by the Dorsetshire Regiment monument on the right at the next road junction.   From here, on a clear day, there is a fine view of Caen.

To your half-right is Maltot.   Battalions of tanks and infantry from Hampshire and Dorset were decimated in the fields ahead of you as they made for the village in the thrust of 10th July.

LINKS (refer to main tour page for time required to finish)

FULL A, B, E, G, H, J, K, L: Continue straight on along the D8 and at the N175 turn left.   After half a mile (1km) turn right following the sign to **Boulevard Périphérique**.   At the next junction, don't follow signs to Cherbourg/St. Lo, but turn off right to **Autres Directions**.   You will shortly see signs to **Mémorial** (the name of the museum).   Follow these signs all the way to the museum and park in the car park. **[10m, 16km: 0h 30m].**   Now follow the CAEN MODULE (page 53).

FULL C, I: Turn immediately right onto the D36 and then left onto the D89 to **Vieux**.   Here turn left to **Feuguerolles-Bully**.   Continue along the D89 over the River Orne *(one of the objectives of EPSOM not achieved)* and straight through St. André-sur-Orne and St. Martin-de-Fontenay.   Carry on and, at the flyover, take the N158 **Falaise** road.   On the N158 stop on the verge just before a turning under the power lines (to Rocquancourt). **[8m, 13km: 0h 25m].**   Now follow the TOTALISE - SOUTHBOUND MODULE (page 67).

FULL D: Continue straight on along the D8 and at the N175 turn left.   After half a mile (1km) turn right following the sign to **Boulevard Périphérique**.   At the next junction follow signs to **Cherbourg/St. Lo**.   This is the N13.   When the N13 arrives in **Bayeux**, at the ring road turn right signposted **Cherbourg**.   Continue for 1.25m (2km) and turn right signposted **Longues**.   At Longues, carry straight over to the **Batteries** and park. **[26m, 42km: 1h 0m].**   Now follow the OMAHA - WESTBOUND MODULE (page 20).

FULL F: Follow Full D (above) to the **Bayeux** ring road, then turn left signposted **St. Lo**.   Continue on the ring road for just over a mile (2km) and you will see the museum on your right. **[22m, 35km: 0h 50m].**   Now follow the BAYEUX MODULE (page 23).

CAEN MODULE

Begins and ends: Musée Mémorial just off the N413 ring road NW of Caen (with city visit option).
[City option ending: Abbaye-aux-Hommes in the west of Caen city centre, SW of the castle.]

Total distance:	None (City glimpse 8m, 12km)	) excluding
Estimated time (hr:min):	Visits 2:00 (City glimpse: Travel 1:00)	) the link

Your tour will have brought you to the car park of the Memorial Museum (Musée Mémorial - la musée pour la paix - the museum for peace).

The people of Caen suffered terribly in 1944. Although the Allies had planned to liberate the city on D-Day, it was not until a month later, 9th July, that the north part was freed from four years of German occupation - and another month before they were finally expelled. But at a terrible cost - they were bombed, bombed and bombed again - over 1,000 times! Six thousand civilians were killed outright or entombed in the rubble and thousands were injured. On 7th July a thousand RAF bombers dropped their deadly loads for 45 minutes on a city that was already three-quarters flattened. As the Germans moved south of the River Orne over the next two days, the British and Canadian troops cautiously moved in and were appalled at the sight that met their eyes. And yet they were warmly welcomed by the people who were able to forgive them for the carnage, as peace returned to this old city. And it was their desire for continued peace that prompted the creation of the Musée pour la Paix.

Visit the museum and see one or more of the excellent films [2 hours].

The module and timing for your tour end here. If you do not wish to see Caen, follow the LINKS (FROM THE MUSEUM) on page 58.

OPTIONAL

However, if you wish to brave the Caen traffic and see something of this splendid city, you have two options, either to take a short drive to GLIMPSE the city or to drive in, PARK and do what you wish. The former will take about an hour, the latter is up to you. Don't rush with the traffic. Stop where you can to admire the lovely buildings.

If you wish to park, it is recommended that you first follow the GLIMPSE tour to get your bearings. Then park and visit the Tourist Office (**Office de Tourisme**) in Rue St. Jean, opposite St. Pierre church, to find out what to see.

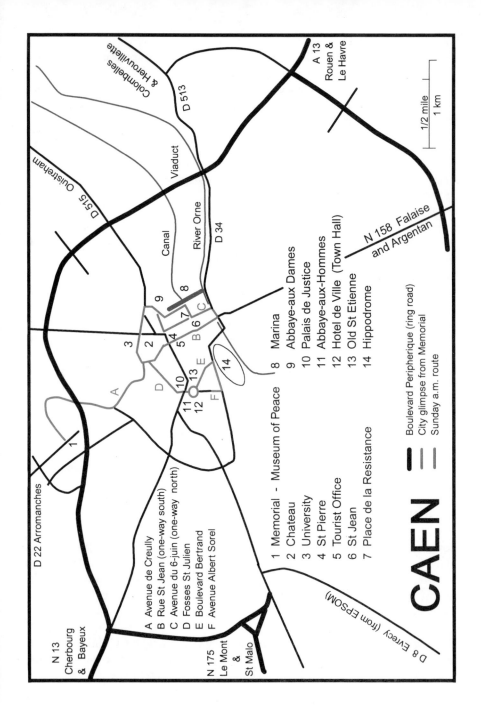

CAEN

A Avenue de Creully
B Rue St Jean (one-way south)
C Avenue du 6-juin (one-way north)
D Fosses St Julien
E Boulevard Bertrand
F Avenue Albert Sorel

1 Memorial - Museum of Peace
2 Chateau
3 University
4 St Pierre
5 Tourist Office
6 St Jean
7 Place de la Resistance
8 Marina
9 Abbaye-aux Dames
10 Palais de Justice
11 Abbaye-aux-Hommes
12 Hotel de Ville (Town Hall)
13 Old St Etienne
14 Hippodrome

━━━ Boulevard Peripherique (ring road)
═══ City glimpse from Memorial
      Sunday a.m. route

N 13 Cherbourg & Bayeux
D 22 Arromanches
N 175 Le Mont & St Malo
D 8 Evrecy (from EPSOM)
D 515 Ouistreham
Colombelles & Herouvillette
D 513
Viaduct
Canal
River Orne
D 34
N 158 Falaise and Argentan
A 13 Rouen & Le Havre

1/2 mile
1 km

We will be going into the city, will circle the chateau (a good place to ask for, if you get lost), passing the fine St Pierre church, then drive straight through the city (south) and across the River Orne. Back north over the river, we will see the Place de la Résistance, which was named in memory of those brave French men and women who aided the Allies with acts of sabotage. We will pass along the Port de Plaisance (the marina), see the Abbaye-aux-Dames (Abbey for Women) created by William the Conqueror's wife Mathilde and then the Abbaye-aux-Hommes (Abbey for Men) with its beautiful neighbour, the Hôtel de Ville (Town Hall). 10,000 people sheltered in the Abbaye-aux-Hommes during the bombing and survived as, remarkably, it was not hit. Opposite you will see the ruins of St. Etienne church left as it was in 1944 in memory of the people of Caen who died during these terrible months. After a drive past the Prairie Hippodrome, the trotting stadium, we will stop to gather ourselves for the required LINK to the next module - these start at the mini-roundabout by the Abbaye-aux-Hommes in front of the Palais de Justice.

TO GLIMPSE

Turn right out of the museum car park, then immediately left. From here follow signs all the way to **Centre Ville** or **Caen-Centre**. As you go under the ring road, move into the left lane ready to turn left at the second of a pair of traffic lights, signposted (on the right) **Jardin des Plantes** and (in the left turning) **Centre Ville**. This road (**Avenue de Creully**) takes you down to the 11th century castle (the traffic is one-way on many roads and here goes anti-clockwise around the castle). Move over to the left lane and hug the left hand side (don't worry about left-P-arrows on the road). You will see the castle walls to your left and the fine church of **St. Pierre** ahead. Turn left at the lights and continue to hug the left side.

[Those on Full D, E, F and H should notice the fork right to Ouistreham Ferry that they will be taking later.]

Turn left at the next two sets of lights and as you reach the crest of the hill, the entrance to the **chateau** is to your left and the **university** is to your right.

As you descend the hill (ahead is the road you came in on), move into the second lane as you bear left.

[Notice a turning off to the right signposted Hotel de Ville and Abbaye-aux-Hommes - we will be going up there later.]

Keep in the second lane from the left to go straight over when you again reach the St. Pierre traffic lights. This is the one-way **Rue St. Jean** (the church straight ahead of you). Immediately to your right, looking at St. Pierre, is the **Tourist Office**.

Go right down Rue St. Jean and as you cross the river, keep left as you will turn immediately left on the other side (still one-way!).

This is the side that was still held by the Germans after the north side had been liberated.

Turn left over the next bridge (**Pont Churchill**) becoming the one-way **Avenue du 6-juin**. Move into the right lane, ready to turn right **this side** of the **Place de la Résistance** (with its gold statue of Joan of Arc amid trees).

[Every Sunday morning there is a market in the Place Courtonne and it is closed to traffic from 8 p.m. on Saturday until 2 p.m. on Sunday. If you are there at that time, continue up Avenue du 6-juin and at the last lights before the castle, turn right. Now miss out the next paragraph and continue.]

Having turned right, carry straight on till you reach the marina with its expensive yachts, where you turn left alongside it towards the **Place Courtonne** (a good parking spot for later, close to St Pierre). Turn right across the end of the marina, go straight ahead (to the left of the Hotel Ibis) and turn right at the T-junction.

Fork left at the roundabout up the hill. To your right is the Eglise de la Trinité with the **Abbaye-aux-Dames** behind.

Go around the roundabout in front of the Abbaye, then file into the single track on the left of the road leading to the main road ahead, signed **Centre Ville**. Turn left and you will reach the familiar crossroads with the hill ahead leading up to the university and the chateau entrance.

Go ahead up and down the hill, but this time move over to the 3rd lane as we will now be taking the right turn to **Abbaye-aux-Hommes**, which you will see in the distance.

Drive straight along, passing close to the equestrian statue. Bear sharp left with the road (don't go straight on to the Abbaye) and at the mini-roundabout bear right.

Keep over to the left here with the aim of moving between two sets of kerbstones to hug the roundabout on your left.

Drive around the roundabout as many times as you like, admiring the big square **Hôtel-de-Ville** (Town Hall), the **Abbaye** to the right of it, the ruined **St. Etienne** church opposite and, beyond the mini-roundabout you just crossed, the **Palais de Justice**.

When you are ready, take the road directly opposite the Hôtel de Ville. This is the **Boulevard Bertrand** which will take you down to the **Place Gambetta**. Follow the road around to the left, then keep in the right lane at the lights (avoiding the bus lane). Turn right here (but wait for buses going **straight on** in the bus lane) into **Rue Sadi Carnot**. Turn right at the next lights and you will see the **Prairie Hippodrome** to your left.

At the second set of lights, turn right again into **Avenue Albert-Sorel** where you will see the Palais de Justice ahead of you. Stop as soon as you can.

Now choose your LINK (FROM THE ABBAYE) on page 59 and follow it or, if you've decided to see more of Caen, read the TO PARK section below.

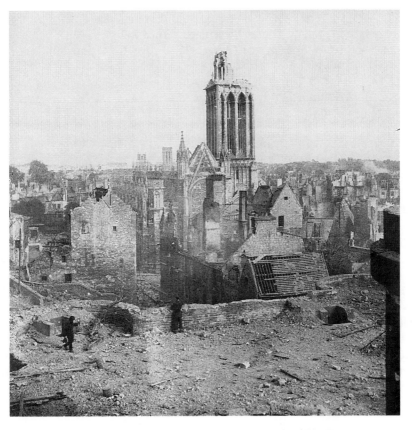

Caen: St. Pierre church from the Chateau ramparts in 1944 [IWM]

TO PARK

There are many car parks as you will have no doubt seen, such as around the chateau and in the Place Courtonne at the end of the marina (you can get there again by going down the **Rue St. Jean** and taking the third left - **Rue de Bernières**).

There is street meter parking everywhere - free from 7 p.m. on Saturday to 10 a.m. on Monday. There are also several underground car parks, such as the **Place de la République**, which is a little way SW of the Tourist Office (beware - they close on Sundays and holidays and you must pay before you return to your car).

LINKS (refer to main tour page for time required to finish)

FROM THE MUSEUM

BASIC A, B, C: Turn right out of the car park, then immediately left. At the next two roundabouts, follow **Toutes Directions**. Then follow the **A13** sign onto the ring road and return to main tour (A page 75, B page 78, C page 80).

FULL A: Turn left out of the car park to the roundabout and join the D22 signposted **Arromanches** (now follow the Abbaye LINK on page 59). **[16m, 26m: 0h 40m].**

FULL B, G, H, J, K, L: Turn right out of the car park, then immediately left. At the next two roundabouts, follow **Toutes Directions**. Then follow the **A13** sign onto the ring road going left (east) and after the viaduct in 3m (5km) turn off onto the D34/513 signposted **Mondeville** (now follow the Abbaye LINK on page 60). **[10m, 16km: 0h 25m].**

FULL C, I/BASIC G: Turn right out of the car park, then immediately left. At the next two roundabouts, follow **Toutes Directions**. Then follow the **Cherbourg** sign onto the ring road going right (west) and continue straight on to join the N13 to **Bayeux** (now follow the Abbaye LINK on page 60). **[18m, 29km: 0h 35m].**

TOUR D, F/BASIC E, H: Turn right out of the car park, then immediately left. At the next two roundabouts, follow **Toutes Directions**. Then follow the **A13** sign onto the ring road going left (east) and after 2m (3km) turn off onto the D515 signposted **Ouistreham** (now follow the Abbaye LINK on page 60). **[9m, 14km: 0h 20m].**

FULL E/BASIC J: Follow "Tour D, F" above, then continue all the way to **Ouistreham**. Then return to main tour (E page 87, J page 98). **[11m, 18km: 0h 25m]**.

BASIC I, L: Turn right out of the car park, then immediately left. At the next two roundabouts, follow **Toutes Directions**. Then initially follow the **Cherbourg** sign onto the ring road going right (west) and return to main tour (I page 94, L page 102).

BASIC K: Follow "Full D, F, H" above, then continue direct to **Ouistreham** (now follow the Abbaye LINK on page 60). **[13m, 21km: 0h 40m]**.

FROM THE ABBAYE

BASIC A, B, C: Drive on and, at the roundabout, turn right down the **Boulevard Bertrand**, around the **Place Gambetta** and right at the lights. This time don't turn right to the Prairie, but carry on down, keeping in the middle lane as you cross the river. On the far side bear left, keeping on the right, and at the T-junction turn right under the railway to join the **Alençon/Le Mans** road (N158). Return to main tour (A page 75, B page 78, C page 80).

FULL A: Drive on, around the roundabout, turning left at the mini-roundabout (i.e. next to the Abbaye) onto the D9 **Bayeux** road until the next major junction when you turn right, signposted **Autres Directions**, and after 0.5m (0.8km) move into the left lane (under a white sign to **Le Chemin Vert**) and turn left, signed **Arromanches**. At the top of the hill go straight across, then follow the D22 to **Arromanches**. On the way you will pass through **Creully**, where your road takes a sharp right after the church and descends a hill. Stop at the Dragoon Guards memorial. Read the plaque and look back up at the castle just above the mill.
This was used by broadcasters as a radio station during the campaign and visits may be made by special request.
When you drive off over the River Seulles you will see a chateau to your half left. General Montgomery's headquarters throughout much of the Normandy campaign was encamped in the grounds.
Cross over the D12 and follow the D65 to **Arromanches**. As you descend the hill out of Crépon, you will see the Mulberry Harbour at Arromanches in the distance. At Arromanches, follow signs to **Musée du Débarquement** and park near the museum. **[19m, 31km: 0h 55m]**. Now follow the GOLD - EASTBOUND MODULE (page 26).

FULL B, G, H, J, K, L: Drive on and, at the roundabout, turn right down the **Boulevard Bertrand**, around the **Place Gambetta** and right at the lights.   This time don't turn right to the Prairie but carry on down, keeping in the left lane as you cross the river (one way street).   On the far side, turn left along the riverside on the D34/513, signposted **Mondeville**, that will lead you to **Colombelles** and **Hérouvillette** (don't confuse this with Hérouville!).   Just before Hérouvillette turn right onto the D37 to **Escoville**.   In the centre, turn right (slightly hidden) signposted **Touffreville/Sonnerville** and, at the end of the houses, park on the verge in the avenue of trees. **[9m, 14km: 0h 25m].**   Now follow the GOODWOOD - SOUTHBOUND MODULE (page 61).

FULL C, I/BASIC G: Drive on, around the roundabout, turning left at the mini-roundabout (i.e. next to the Abbaye) onto the D9 **Bayeux** road.   Keep straight along on that road until it joins the N13 to Bayeux (there is a lack of signposts here, but fork right when the left fork goes to Carpiquet).   At the Bayeux ring road, turn left signposted **St Lo**.   Continue on the ring road for 1.25m (2km) and you will see the museum on your right, where you should park. **[18m, 29km: 0h 45m].**   Now follow the BAYEUX MODULE (page 23).

TOUR D, F/BASIC E, H: Drive on around the roundabout and, at the mini-roundabout, go opposite just to the left of the **Palais de Justice** and return to the **chateau**.   Keep left round the chateau (with St Pierre on your right).   At the next fork, fork right signposted **Ouistreham** then keep straight on under the ring road onto the D515.   Turn off at the signpost to **Bénouville**, then at a crossroads turn right onto the D514 signposted **Ranville**.   **Pegasus Bridge** is just ahead of you. Park just before the bridge. **[7m, 11km: 0h 25m].**   Now follow the PEGASUS MODULE (page 40).

FULL E/BASIC J: Follow "Tour D, F" above but don't turn off to Bénouville. Continue instead to **Ouistreham**.   Return to main tour (E page 87, J page 98). **[10m, 16km: 0h 30m].**

BASIC I, L: Drive on, around the roundabout, turning left at the mini-roundabout (i.e. next to the Abbaye) onto the D9 **Bayeux** road.   Very shortly, turn left signposted **Avranches** (N175).   Return to main tour (I page 94, L page 102).

BASIC K: Follow "Tour D, F" above, but don't turn off to Bénouville.   Continue instead to **Ouistreham**.   Just before the ferry terminal keep to the left lane, following signs to the **Plage** (beach).   Carry on until you reach a large building on the right, called **Queen Normandy**.   This is the casino and on your left is the **No. 4 Commando Museum**.   Park on the right, opposite the museum. **[12m, 19km: 0h 40m].**   Now follow the GOLD-WESTBOUND MODULE (page 34).

GOODWOOD - SOUTHBOUND MODULE

Begins: Escoville 6m (10km) NE of Caen.

Ends: Bourgébus just east of the N158 4m (7km) south of Caen.

Total distance: 9m (14km)   )   excluding

Estimated time: (hr:min) Travel 0:45 + Visits 0:00 = Total 0:45   )   the link

Your tour will have brought you just south of Escoville, in an avenue of trees.

By the middle of July, with southern Caen (to your right) still in German hands, General Montgomery decided to make an attempt to break through east of the city, destroying German armour and personnel as much as possible in the process, as a prelude to further advances. They called it Operation Goodwood. As you can see, the area was relatively flat but was overlooked by German positions a mile and a half on either side of the planned route - in the industrial area on the outskirts of Caen to your right and in the woods on the high ground to your left. The target was the ridge at Bourgébus, six miles ahead of you to the south.

In the night of 17th/18th July, 1,000 troop carriers and 900 tanks crossed the Caen canal and the adjacent River Orne over the bridges at Bénouville and Ranville and by two other pairs of temporary bridges close by. At 5 a.m., 1,000 British and American bombers, 400 artillery guns (some in Caen) and three ships at sea sent bombs and shells smashing into the German positions. The bombs that dropped on the valley floor were so fused that they exploded above the ground and caused great damage but left no craters. This enabled the tanks and infantry to make their way south.

By the end of the day they had reached Bourgébus but had to pull back under withering fire from guns on the ridge, which had not been bombed due to shortage of aircraft, nor shelled as it was beyond the Allied artillery range. Only rockets from Typhoon aircraft were available, but the Germans were well hidden in sunken lanes and in the woods to the east and were difficult to find. The next day 19th July, Canadian infantry cleared the southern part of Caen and assisted the British in attacking the ridge again but heavy rain on 20th put a stop to any further attempts for over two weeks.

Remarkably the Allies lost but 100 dead as against many hundred Germans who were killed in the bombing and the subsequent battle: but Montgomery's aim of destroying their armour resulted in two hundred of his own tanks being destroyed whilst the Germans lost only half that number.

Drive on, turning right towards Cuverville. Stop just after the silos.
The start-line was between Escoville and the village to your right, St Honorine-la-Chardonnerette. At this point you are crossing the path that the tanks and infantry took after the whole area, including the villages you are about to pass through, had been bombed.

Ahead is the metal works at Colombelles and behind to your left is the ridge, from both of which the Germans poured shells onto the passing army. In the distance, to the left, is the Bourgébus ridge.

Drive into Cuverville, turn left then immediately right. Stop as soon as the houses end and you can see fields to the left.

While the tanks carried on in the open ground to your left, the infantry followed behind (along your road), clearing the enemy out of the villages. Cuverville was captured by 8.30 and fifty Germans, still stunned by the ferocious bombing, were captured in the trees to your left.

Carry on to **Démouville** and as you leave the village watch out for the church from which snipers fired at the approaching troops. Just before the village end-sign, park on the right.

You are now standing on the track of the old Caen to Troarn railway line that was one of the obstacles for the tanks. They had to take the embankments at an angle to avoid their bellies being perfect targets for the enemy anti-tank guns ahead.

Drive on straight over the N175 towards **Cagny**, imagining yourself to be one of the 64 tanks in the leading wave. Having crossed the flyover above the autoroute (it was not there then) you will shortly draw level with a small hamlet across the field to your right. Stop well after the bend (for safety's sake).

All the tanks passed through the half-mile gap between here and Cagny ahead and were savagely attacked by anti-tank guns sitting in the trees to the left of the village. Twelve British tanks were destroyed within seconds. Cagny itself had been obliterated by the Allied bombardment. German tanks counter-attacked at one point from the woods a mile (2km) to your left but all but one were destroyed.

Carry on to Cagny, turn left on the N13 towards **Lisieux** and at the roundabout turn right onto the D225 to **Bourgébus**.

As you cross the open fields, look left up to the ridge where the Germans were hidden in the woods and villages.

Continue on to **Soliers**, where you turn left at the church and bear left at the roundabout to **Bourgébus**.

At Bourgébus, turn right signposted **Hubert-Folie** (Rue des Canadiens). Just after the village-end sign, go over the railway and pause (well beyond the bridge, for safety) by the side of the road.

From here you will see the field of fire that the Germans possessed that forced the British tanks to hold back at Bras to the left of the ridge and at Soliers ahead. Trying to cross the railway (a mining line running down to the quarries near Falaise) caused them great difficulties, as you can imagine.

LINKS (refer to main tour page for time required to finish)

FULL A, B, G, H, J, K, L: Continue on across the flyover, and turn immediately right signposted N158 **Falaise**. Having joined the main road, stop on the verge just before a turning under the power-lines (to Rocquancourt). **[2m, 3km: 0h 10m].** Now follow the TOTALISE - SOUTHBOUND MODULE (page 67).

FULL C, I: Continue on and turn right onto the N158 towards **Caen** for 1.5m (3km) then turn right at the roundabout onto the Caen ring road (signposted **Cherbourg**). After 2m (3km) turn right at the second interchange (coming very soon after the first) onto the D513, following signs to **Cherbourg**. After 4m (6km) you will see signs for **Mémorial** (the name of the museum). Turn off here, follow further signs to **Mémorial** and park in the car park. **[11m, 18km: 0h 25m].** Now follow the CAEN MODULE (page 53).

GOODWOOD - NORTHBOUND MODULE

Begins: Bourgébus 4m (7km) south of Caen.
Ends: Cuverville 4m (7km) east of Caen.

Total distance: 8m (13km)) excluding
Estimated time (hr:min): Travel 0:40 + Visits 0:0 = Total 0:40) the link

Your tour will have brought you by the railway bridge in Bourgébus.

By the middle of July, with southern Caen still in German hands, General Montgomery decided to make an attempt to break through east of the city, destroying German armour and personnel as much as possible in the process, as a prelude to further advances. They called it Operation Goodwood. As you can see, the area was relatively flat but was overlooked by German positions a mile and a half on either side of the planned route - in the industrial area on the outskirts of Caen to your left and in the woods on the high ground to your right. The target was the ridge you are now on, six miles to the south of the start-line.

In the night of 17th/18th July, 1,000 troop carriers and 900 tanks crossed the Caen canal and the adjacent River Orne over the bridges at Bénouville and Ranville and by two other pairs of temporary bridges close by. At 5 a.m., 1,000 British and American bombers, 400 artillery guns (some in Caen) and three ships at sea sent bombs and shells smashing into the German positions. The bombs that dropped on the valley floor were so fused that they exploded above the ground and caused great damage but left no craters. This enabled the tanks and infantry to make their way south.

By the end of the day they had reached Bourgébus but had to pull back under withering fire from guns on the ridge, which had not been bombed due to shortage of aircraft, nor shelled as it was beyond the Allied artillery range. Only rockets from Typhoon aircraft were available, but the Germans were well hidden in sunken lanes and in the woods over to your right and were difficult to find. The next day, 19th July, Canadian infantry cleared the southern part of Caen and assisted the British in attacking the ridge again but heavy rain on 20th put a stop to any further attempts for over two weeks.

Remarkably the Allies lost but 100 dead as against many hundred Germans who were killed in the bombing and the subsequent battle: but Montgomery's aim of destroying their armour resulted in two hundred of his own tanks being destroyed whilst the Germans lost only half that number.

From here you will see the field of fire that the Germans possessed that forced the British tanks to hold back at Bras to the left of the ridge and at Soliers ahead.

Trying to cross the railway (a mining line running down to the quarries near Falaise) caused them great difficulties, as you can imagine.

Drive on and turn left to **Soliers**. After the roundabout in Soliers, take the first right at the church (signposted **Cagny** on the nearside).

As you cross the open fields, look back to the right to see the woods where the Germans were hidden.

Carry on to a roundabout and turn left on the N13 to **Cagny** (which was obliterated by the bombing). At Cagny church turn right onto the D228 (**Démouville**), but stop at the end of the houses.

All the British tanks passed through the half-mile gap between here and the hamlet to your half-left, Le Mesnil Frémentel. They were savagely attacked by anti-tank guns in the trees behind to your right. Twelve tanks were destroyed within seconds. German tanks counter-attacked at one point from the woods a mile to your right, but all but one were destroyed.

Carry on across the tanks' path towards Démouville (across the flyover above the autoroute which was not there then) but stop on the verge immediately after the N175 crossroads, just in front of the village sign.

You are now standing on the track of the old Caen to Troarn railway line that was another obstacle for the tanks. They had to take the embankments at an angle to avoid their bellies being perfect targets for the enemy anti-tank guns behind you.

As the tanks came down towards you on the open ground to your right, the infantry followed behind, along your road, clearing the enemy out of the villages. As you enter Démouville you will see the church from which snipers fired at the approaching troops and, just before Cuverville, the woods to your right where fifty Germans, still stunned from the ferocious bombing, were captured.

Drive on and at **Cuverville** turn left then immediately right and stop before you reach the silos. Turn the car around.

The start-line for Operation Goodwood was between St Honorine-en-Chardonnerette on your right and Escoville behind to your right. You will see ahead the metal works at Colombelles and behind (to your left) the ridge, from both of which the Germans poured shells onto the tanks and infantry as they passed this very spot on their way to the Bourgébus ridge that you can see in the distance to your half-left.

Drive back into Cuverville and turn right onto the D226.

LINKS (refer to main tour page for time required to finish)

FULL D, F: Carry on along the D226 to the crossroads and turn left onto the D513, signposted **Caen**. Just before the viaduct, keep in the left lane to turn left onto the ring road signposted **Cherbourg**. After 3m (5km) you will see signs for **Mémorial** (the name of the museum). Turn off here, follow further signs to **Mémorial** and park in the car park. **[7m, 11km: 0h 15m].** Now follow the CAEN MODULE (page 53).

FULL E: Carry on along the D226 over the crossroads signposted **Ouistreham** and having crossed the Orne river, a roundabout and the Caen canal, turn right onto the D515 signposted **Ouistreham**. Turn off at the signpost to **Bénouville**, then at a crossroads turn right onto the D514 signposted **Ranville**. **Pegasus Bridge** is just ahead of you. Park just before the bridge. **[7m, 11km: 0h 20m].** Now follow the PEGASUS MODULE (page 40).

TOTALISE - SOUTHBOUND MODULE

Begins: At N158/D230 junction near Rocquancourt (5m, 8km, south of Caen).
Ends: August 1944 Museum in Falaise 21m (34km) south of Caen.

Total distance: 22m (35km)) excluding
Estimated time (hr:min): Travel 1:00 + Visits 1:15 = Total 2:15) the link

Your tour will have brought you onto the N158, the road from Caen to Falaise, parked on the verge just before a small turning to Rocquancourt under the power lines 3m (5km) south of the Caen ring road.

OPERATION TOTALISE

From 20th July, when Operation Goodwood was halted south-east of Caen, British and Canadian forces kept the German defenders occupied in and around the many villages south of Caen. Then just before midnight on 7th August, 400 Canadian tanks, supported by infantry (carried in specially armoured vehicles nicknamed "Kangaroos"), formed up in four columns on either side of the road you are now on and rushed towards Falaise. They were preceded by 500 American Flying Fortresses which dropped 3,500 tons of bombs on the path ahead of them

At first all went well, helped by the fact that much of the German tank force had been sent to the west in an attempt to stem the tide of Americans sweeping eastwards from Avranches. They then met the full force of the Tigers, those mighty tanks that were far superior in armament and armour-plating to any of the Allied tanks, and the southwards dash of the liberating forces was halted.

The next day, at noon, two fresh divisions, one Canadian and one Polish, sped through the front line, again preceded by American bombers. Unfortunately, as happened so often in Normandy, several bombs fell short, killing 200 Allied men and wounding a Canadian General. But the new divisions carried on and achieved another two miles before they were stopped again, at Cintheaux.

[About 3m (5km) from here, there is a **Canadian war cemetery** which used to have access from the road. It is now blocked off and one has to take a detour through **Cintheaux** - a round-trip of 5m (8km), taking 15 minutes, plus the time you spend at the cemetery. This is **not** included in the timing for this tour, but if you wish to visit it, watch out for the green signpost in 2m (3km). Return over the N158 then turn right to **Falaise** to rejoin the main road.]

Drive on, noticing the villages on either side that were totally destroyed by the preliminary bombing.

Notice the Canadian cemetery off to your right if you don't choose to visit it and after a further 2.5 miles (4km), you will see a **Polish war cemetery** also on the right. Park in the lay-by and visit the cemetery [15 mins].

Return to the car. *One notable event at this time was the destruction of the Tiger tank containing the most successful panzer commander in Normandy, Michael Wittmann. In typical style he attempted to attack five Canadian Sherman tanks single-handed, but with brilliant co-ordinated fire, they blew his tank to pieces. This achievement was soon outweighed by a panzer division of Hitler Youth, the most determined and dangerous troops in the German army, which struck at an isolated Canadian column near Estrées-la-Campagne and knocked out 47 tanks and two companies of infantry.*

Drive on and very soon take the second turning left in **Langannerie** onto the D131 to **Estrées-la-Campagne**. Go through the village and after 2m (3km) stop at the monument in some trees on the right. This is the very spot where the Canadian tanks were destroyed by the Panzers of the Hitler Youth who were in the wood behind the monument. Read the plaque.

Turn around at the road junction just ahead and in Estrées turn left onto the D260 signposted **Soumont**, fork right at the village-end sign and stop just before rejoining the N158.

OPERATION TRACTABLE

"Totalise" was halted near Estrées on 11th August with seven miles to Falaise still to go. Success came three days later when "Operation Tractable" sent more fresh forces against the wilting Germans. The same pattern of parallel columns preceded by 800 bombers again met with disaster as bombs fell short and killed 150 Allied soldiers. At this point the Hitler Youth panzer division was withdrawn and many of the less enthusiastic tank crews and infantry surrendered to the Canadian and Polish forces. Meanwhile the remains of Wittmann's Tiger battalion valiantly tried to hold back the opposing forces to enable the Germans to retreat towards the east, as the Americans began to close in from the south at Argentan.

On 15th August the Polish Armoured Division had the satisfaction of clearing Potigny many of whose inhabitants were miners of Polish extraction. As they continued on, with the Canadians off to the left streaming through the cornfields, there came into sight at last the battlements of the castle at Falaise, birthplace of William the Conqueror.

In two days, on 17th, Falaise fell to the Canadians. The mighty German army, worn out by two months of bitter fighting, with their tanks and transport in disrepair and short of fuel, decided it was time to go. In the High School at Falaise, 60 grenadiers of the Hitler Youth in typically defiant mood chose not to retreat, refused to surrender and died together in a last ditch stand.

The Battle for Normandy had been won by the Allies and its liberation was about to be completed.

[Northbound readers should now return to page 70.]

Turn left onto the N158 and as you start to by-pass the town of **Potigny** you can see the old mines off to the right. Carry on and look for the first sight of Falaise, so yearned for by the Allied troops after 10 days of hard fighting. The road descends on entering **Falaise** and, as the road bears left and starts climbing into the town, look right along the valley at the mighty walls of William's castle to your right. You will also see why Falaise (meaning "cliff") was given its name.

If the **August 1944 Museum** is advertised as being open at the time of your visit (see Musée Août 1944 opening times on page 111, but don't rely on them!), turn right by a car park onto the **Vire** road and you will see the circular building in a small valley a very short distance behind the castle on your right.

Drive down into the car park and visit the museum [1 hour].

If it is not open, follow your next link below.

LINKS (refer to main tour page for time required to finish).

BASIC A, B, C: [Those on the Basic Tour who chose to follow the TOTALISE - SOUTHBOUND MODULE may either return to their main tour and drive to Argentan (A page 75, B page 78, C page 80) or follow the road described below to drive the FALAISE POCKET MODULE.]

FULL A, B, C, G, H, I, J, K, L: From the museum drive back to the main road in Falaise and turn right. Ignore lorry signs turning left to Trun, but very shortly, at some triangles of grass, you will see a signpost to **Trun** to the **right**. This will take you in a semicircle back across the main road to a road opposite. This will lead you onto the D63 which becomes the D13 to Trun. Drive through the village, signposted **St Lambert** and, after the first hill, park on the verge when you can see the river valley ahead. **[14m, 23km: 0h 35m].** Now follow the FALAISE POCKET MODULE (page 72).

TOTALISE - NORTHBOUND MODULE

Begins: August 1944 Museum in Falaise 21m (34km) south of Caen.

Ends: Polish war cemetery at Grainville-Langannerie mid-way between Caen and Falaise on the N158.

Total distance: 16m (26km)) excluding
Estimated time (hr:min): Travel 0:50 + Visits 1:15 = Total 2:05) the link

Your tour will have brought you to the car park of the August 1944 Museum at Falaise or, if it is closed, on the main road through Falaise.

If open, visit the museum [1 hour]. Drive back to the main road through Falaise and turn left onto the N158 towards **Caen**.

As the road descends out of the town and bears right, look left along the valley at the mighty walls of William's castle. You will also see why Falaise (meaning "cliff") was given its name.

Continue up the hill and when you reach the end of the houses and trees, stop on the verge overlooking fields on either side.

[As you are travelling in the opposite direction to the Allied advance, you unfortunately cannot read the battle-story as-you-go. Turn to page 67 and read all three sections in italics in the Southbound Module then return to this page.]

Drive on and 1m (2km) after by-passing the mining town of **Potigny** (notice the old mines on the left at the end of the by-pass), turn right opposite a silo onto the D260 to **Estrées-la-Campagne**. In Estrées, turn right onto the D131 and after 2m (3km) stop at the monument in some trees on the right.

This is the very spot where the 47 Canadian tanks were destroyed by the Panzers of the Hitler Youth who were in the wood behind the monument. Read the plaque.

Turn around at the road junction just ahead and carry straight on through Estrées, keeping to the D131 to **Langannerie** where you turn right, back onto the N158.

After 0.4m (0.6km) stop in the lay-by opposite the **Polish war cemetery**. Take great care crossing the road and visit the cemetery [15 mins].

[About 2.5 miles (4 km) from here, there is a **Canadian war cemetery** which used to have access from this road. It is now blocked off and one has to take a detour through **Cintheaux** - a round-trip of 5 miles (8km), taking 15 minutes, plus the time you spend at the cemetery. This is **not** included in the timing for this tour, but if you wish to visit it, watch out for the green signpost in 1m (2km). Return over the N158 then turn left to rejoin the main road to Caen.]

LINKS (refer to main tour page for time required to finish)

BASIC D, E, F: Return to main tour (D page 83, E page 86, F page 88).
[If, however, you wish to follow the CAEN MODULE (which is **not** included in the Basic Tour timing), continue north from the Polish Cemetery and after 9m (14km) turn right at the roundabout onto the Caen ring road (signposted **Cherbourg**). After 2m (3 km) turn right at the second interchange (coming very soon after the first) onto the D513, following signs to **Cherbourg**. After 4m (6km) you will see signs to **Mémorial** (the name of the museum). Turn off here, follow further signs to **Mémorial** and park in the car park. **[16m, 26km: 0h 30m].** Now follow the CAEN MODULE (page 53).]

FULL D, E, F: From the Polish cemetery continue north towards **Caen** noticing Cintheaux and other villages to your left and to your right which were flattened by the Allied bombing and by the artillery of both sides. After 6m (10km) watch out for some power lines crossing the road: pass underneath them and after 1m (2km) at a flyover turn right onto the D89 to **Bourgébus**. Go over the railway bridge and stop on the verge at the end of the grass bank before the houses start. **[8m, 13km: 0h 20m].** Now follow the GOODWOOD - NORTHBOUND MODULE (page 64).

FALAISE POCKET MODULE

Begins: Just SE of Trun (on the D13 11m, 18km, east of Falaise and on the D916 8m, 13km, north east of Argentan).

Ends: Tournai-sur-Dive, a village just south of Trun.

Total distance: 13m (21km)) excluding
Estimated time (hr:min): Travel 0:55 + Visits 0:15 = Total 1:10) the link

Your tour will have brought you 1m (2km) east of Trun, overlooking a river valley.

By August 13th, American forces had taken the Cherbourg peninsula and had fought their way south and then east (south of the British Sector), then moved north to Argentan (see map on page 4). Four days later the Canadians and Poles reached Falaise. Between the two allied forces was a pocket in which the German army fought desperately to move east to avoid a holocaust. Unfortunately for the Allies, the Germans managed to keep the gap open long enough for 50,000 to escape towards the Seine and Germany, but in the process they suffered murderous strafing from Allied aircraft as they struggled along the congested lanes. As a result of this and of shelling from the ground forces, 10,000 were killed and 40,000 captured.

The stretch of road ahead marks the beginning of the area of absolute chaos as the Germans fled up each of the little lanes leading off to your left. The hill ahead is the point reached by the Argyll and Sutherland Highlanders of Canada on the evening of 18th August. From here, they rained heavy fire down on the Germans fleeing in their thousands from right to left through St. Lambert.

Drive on and as you go over the next hill notice what sitting targets the Germans must have been as they struggled through **St. Lambert**. Go through the village and in **Chambois** turn left at the castle onto the D16 towards **Mont Ormel**.

You are now driving along one of the German escape routes and as you climb up the road to Mont Ormel, you will see the monument on the hill ahead which marks the spot from which a Polish regiment fired down onto the fleeing forces. Added to the terror created by the Allied Typhoon aircraft, they created a living hell for Hitler's mighty troops.

Turn left at Mont Ormel signposted to the memorial and after a short distance drive up to the monument on the right.

It commemorated a dreadful fight on August 20th in which bayonets and knives were used in desperate fighting by both sides.

Visit the monument and admire the view [15min].

As you drive out of the car park, turn sharp right along the escarpment. Take the second turning left, signposted **St. Lambert**.

You are now driving in the reverse direction from that taken by the Germans. Notice the overhanging trees under which they attempted to hide from the aircraft and the narrowness of the lane that caused further chaos when tanks and other vehicles broke down or were destroyed.

At St Lambert go straight over the D13 and, a hundred metres past the church, you will pass over the tiny bridge over which the fleeing Germans had to pass. Look up to the right at the hill from which the Canadians were pouring their fire. Continue on to a T-junction. Turn right for **Tournai-sur-Dive** and park in an avenue of trees just short of the village.

From 19th August, this little place was subjected to a 57-hour non-stop artillery attack by the Canadians in an effort to stop the Germans. Both the Germans and French civilians tried desperately to escape the onslaught. Eventually 2,700 Germans surrendered, enabling the Canadians to move into the village and, on the spot you are now sitting, meet up with the Americans who came up from behind you. It was 8 a.m. on 22nd August and the Falaise Gap had been closed!

General Eisenhower, Supreme Commander of "Overlord",
receives a Liberation medal from General de Gaulle [All rights reserved]

LINKS (refer to main tour page for time required to finish)

FULL A, B, C, I, K, L: Return to main tour (A page 76, B page 79, C page 82, I page 96, K page 101, L page 103).

FULL D, E, F: Turn right in Tournai and at the D13 turn left, through **Trun** to **Falaise** where you follow signs to **Autres Directions** and then **Caen**. If the **August 1944 Museum** in Falaise is advertised as being open at the time of your visit (see Musée Août 1944 opening times on page 111, but don't rely on them!), turn left off the main road at a car park onto the **Vire** road and you will see the circular building in a small valley a very short distance behind the castle on your right. Drive down into the museum car park. If it is not open, stay on the main road. **[17m, 27km: 0h 40m].** Now follow the TOTALISE - NORTHBOUND MODULE (page 70).

FULL G, H: Turn right in **Tournai** and at the D13 turn left, through **Trun** to **Falaise**. Here follow signs to **Autres Directions** and then **Caen**. At a roundabout just before Caen, turn right onto the ring road (signposted **Cherbourg**). Immediately after the A13 turning, turn off to **Cherbourg**. At the junction after the viaduct, take the D515 towards **Ouistreham**. After 4m (6km) turn right to **Bénouville**. Carry straight on until you turn right onto the D514 signposted **Ranville**. **Pegasus Bridge** is ahead of you. Park just before the bridge. **[43m, 69km: 1h 15m].** Now follow the PEGASUS MODULE (page 40).

FULL J: Follow "Full G, H" above, but after the viaduct stay on the ring road for 4m (6km) until the turning signposted **Arromanches**. Follow the D22 all the way to Arromanches. On the way you will pass through **Creully**, where your road takes a sharp right after the church and descends a hill. Stop at the Dragoon Guards memorial. Read the plaque and look back up at the castle just above the mill. *This was used by broadcasters as a radio station during the campaign and visits may be made by special request.*
When you drive off over the River Seulles, you will see a chateau to your half left. General Montgomery's headquarters through much of the Normandy campaign was encamped in the grounds.
Cross over the D12 and follow the D65 to **Arromanches**. As you descend the hill out of Crépon, you will see the Mulberry Harbour at Arromanches in the distance. At Arromanches, follow signs to **Musée du Débarquement** and park near the museum. **[58m, 93km: 2h 00m].** Now follow the GOLD - EASTBOUND MODULE (page 26).

TOUR A: DETOUR GOING SOUTH FROM CHERBOURG

Begins: Ferry terminal, Cherbourg.
Ends: Argentan (35m, 56km, south of Caen on the N158).

BASIC TOUR A

		TIME (hr:min)	
		Module	To
Total distance:	182m (293km)	& link	finish
Estimated time (hr:min): Travel 10:10 + Visits 12:00 = Total 22:10			

From the ferry take the road opposite, following signs to **Caen**.
After only 0.8m (1.3km), just after the last traffic lights and
before the hill, there is a turning left signposted (facing the
opposite way!) **Fort du Roule**. This museum is four minutes up
a winding road and if it is open (see Musée de la Guerre et de la
Libération on page 110) spend 30 minutes there.

Continue south on the N13, to **Ste. Mère Eglise**. As you enter
the town, just before the square, turn right signposted **La Poste**
and, on the nearside, **Chef-du-Pont**. Go under the N13, fork
left on the D67 and, just after Chef-du-Pont (2.5m, 4km) as the
river comes into view, park by the memorial on the right.
[28m, 45km: 1h 30m from the ferry].   [1:30] 20:40

Now follow the **STE. MERE MODULE** (page 11).   [2:35] 18:05
This links directly with the following modules:

UTAH - SOUTHBOUND (page 13)	[2:35]	15:30
OMAHA - EASTBOUND (page 17)	[4:40]	10:50
BAYEUX (page 23)	[2:20]	8:30
GOLD - EASTBOUND (page 26)	[5:40]	2:50
PEGASUS (page 40)	[1:40]	1:10

From Pegasus Bridge carry on over the crossroads and over the
bridge, following signs for **Caen** (5m, 8km).

[Here you may wish to visit Caen museum and/or city - this is
NOT included in the timing. To do so, at the ring road turn
right signposted **Cherbourg** then after 2m (3km) turn off at the
sign for **Mémorial** (the name of the museum).   Then follow
further signs to **Mémorial** and park in the car park.   Now
follow the CAEN MODULE (page 53).]

To reach Argentan, at the **Caen** ring road initially follow the sign
to the **A13**, but stay on the ring road until you turn off onto the
N158 to **Falaise** and **Argentan** (36m, 58km from where you
joined the Caen ring road).

[As you will be following the direction of the TOTALISE - SOUTHBOUND MODULE (part of the Full Tour) when you reach the N158 roundabout, you may like to follow that module (see page 67) and also the FALAISE POCKET MODULE that leads on from it (page 72).]

[41m, 66km: 1h 10m from Pegasus Bridge to Argentan, excluding the options in square brackets].   [1:10]   0:00

FULL TOUR A

Total distance:281m (452km)
Estimated time (hr:min):Travel 17:10 + Visits 16:15 = Total 33:25

From the ferry follow the Basic Tour above to **Chef-du-Pont**, but with the following variation:-
A flying bomb (V1) launch site may be seen (but not visited as it is on private land) by turning off the N13 (6m,10km from the ferry terminal) at the sign to **Brix/St. Martin-le-G** then turn left, over the N13 signposted **Le Theil**.   Continue on that road for 2 miles (3km) and the site will be seen quite clearly on your left. *V1s, known as "doodle-bugs" or "buzz-bombs", killed over 5,000 people in England during June and July 1944, injured 35,000 and damaged 30,000 buildings.*
Spend a few minutes there then return to the N13 the way you went. **[32m, 52km: 1h 45m].**   [1:45]   31:40

Now follow the **STE. MERE MODULE** (page 11).   [2:35]   29:05
This links directly with the following modules:

UTAH - SOUTHBOUND (page 13)	[2:35]	26.30
OMAHA - EASTBOUND (page 17)	[4:40]	21:50
BAYEUX (page 23)	[2:15]	19:35
TILLY (page 48)	[0:55]	18:40
EPSOM (page 50)	[1:40]	17:00
CAEN (page 53)	[2:40]	14:20
GOLD - EASTBOUND (page 26)	[5:40]	8:40
PEGASUS (page 40)	[1:40]	7:00
MERVILLE (page 43)	[1:50]	5:10
GOODWOOD - SOUTHBOUND (page 61)	[0:55]	4:15
TOTALISE - SOUTHBOUND (page 67)	[2:50]	1:25
FALAISE POCKET (page 72)	[1:10]	0:15

Drive through the village of **Tournai-sur-Dive** to **Villedieu-lès-Bailleul** and at the D916 turn left for **Argentan**. **[7m, 11km: 0h 15m].**

Royal Marine Commandos land on Sword Beach [IWM]

TOUR B: DETOUR GOING SOUTH FROM OUISTREHAM (CAEN)

Begins: Ferry terminal, Ouistreham (9m, 14km, north of Caen).
Ends: Argentan (35m, 56km, south of Caen on the N158).

[If you are coming from the Channel Tunnel or ports from Le Havre to Calais, refer to page 105.]

BASIC TOUR B

		TIME (hr:min)	
		Module	To
Total distance:	204m (328km)	& link	finish
Estimated time (hr:min):	Travel 10:30 + Visits 11:30 = Total 22:00		

Drive straight out of the ferry terminal following signs firstly to **Autres Directions** and then **Caen**. After 3m (5km) turn off onto the D514 **Bénouville** and **Ranville** (**NOT** the D35 Zone d'Activités de Bénouville) and keep straight on to **Pegasus Bridge**. Park just before the bridge. [4m, 7km: 0h 15m].

[0:15] 21:45

Now follow the **PEGASUS MODULE** (page 40). [2:05] 19:40
This links directly with the following modules:

GOLD - WESTBOUND (page 34)	[5:40]	14:00
OMAHA - WESTBOUND (page 20)	[4:55]	9:05
UTAH - NORTHBOUND (page 15)	[2:05]	7:00
STE. MERE (page 11)	[3:30]	3:30
BAYEUX (page 23)	[2:00]	1:30

From Bayeux museum on the ring road turn left to join the N13 to **Caen** (14m, 23km) where you join the ring road to the left (north) of the city.

[Here you may wish to visit Caen museum and/or city - this is NOT included in the timing. To do so, turn off the ring road to follow signs to **Mémorial** (the name of the museum). Park in the car park and follow the CAEN MODULE (page 53).]

To reach Argentan, stay on the ring road, do **not** follow signs to the A13, but carry on round until you turn off onto the N158 to **Falaise** and **Argentan** (35m, 56km from where you joined the Caen ring road).

[As you will be following the direction of the TOTALISE - SOUTHBOUND MODULE (part of the Full Tour) when you

reach the N158 roundabout, you may like to follow that module
(see page 67) and also the FALAISE POCKET MODULE that
leads on from it (page 72).]

**[55m, 89km: 1h 30m from Bayeux, excluding the options in
square brackets].**

     [1:30]   0:00

FULL TOUR B

Total distance: 285m (459km)
Estimated time (hr:min): Travel 17:10 + Visits 15:30 = Total 32:40

From the ferry follow the Basic Tour (above) to **Pegasus Bridge**.
Park just before the bridge. **[4m, 7km: 0h 15m].**

     [0:15]   32:25

Now follow the **PEGASUS MODULE** (page 40).   [1:40]   30:45
This links directly with the following modules:

	Module & link	To finish
MERVILLE (page 43)	[2:10]	28:35
GOLD - WESTBOUND (page 34)	[5:40]	22:55
OMAHA - WESTBOUND (page 20)	[4:55]	18:00
UTAH - NORTHBOUND (page 15)	[2:05]	15:55
STE. MERE [see NOTE below] (page 11)	[3:30]	12:25
BAYEUX (page 23)	[2:15]	10:10
TILLY (page 48)	[0:55]	9:15
EPSOM (page 50)	[1:40]	7:35
CAEN (page 53)	[2:25]	5:10
GOODWOOD - SOUTHBOUND (page 61)	[0:55]	4:15
TOTALISE - SOUTHBOUND (page 67)	[2:50]	1:25
FALAISE POCKET (page 72)	[1:10]	0:15

Drive through the village of **Tournai-sur-Dive** to
Villedieu-lès-Bailleul and at the D916 turn left for **Argentan**.
[7m, 11km: 0h 15m].

     [0:15]   0:00

[NOTE: An opportunity is given after the Ste. Mère Module to
follow the COBRA MODULE.]

TOUR C: DETOUR GOING SOUTH FROM ST. MALO

Begins: Ferry terminal, St Malo.
Ends: Argentan (35m, 56km, south of Caen on the N158).

[A visit to the town of St Malo is recommended either before you start or when you return - it is NOT included in the timing for this tour.]

BASIC TOUR C

		TIME (hr:min)	
		Module	To
Total distance:	262m (422km)	& link	finish
Estimated time (hr:min): Travel 12:05 + Visits 11:30 = Total 23:35			

From **St. Malo** take the D4 to **Dol de Bretagne** then the N176/175 towards **Avranches** (40m, 65km).

[If you wish to visit **Le Mont St Michel** turn left at **Pontorson** (27m, 43km, from St Malo) and continue for 6 miles (9km). You can rejoin the tour by turning left from Le Mont onto the D275 for **Avranches**. This side-trip is NOT included in the timing.]

Go around the **Avranches** by-pass to **Villedieu-les-Poêles** (14m, 22km). [Poêles means pots and there are many shops in the centre of the town selling copperware - worth a quick visit.] From here follow signs to **St. Lo** (21m, 34km).
[If you wish to follow the short COBRA MODULE (1 hour), follow the FULL TOUR at this point.]
From **St. Lo**, following signs to **Cherbourg**, take the N174/N13 to **Carentan** (20m, 32km). Once past Carentan, 2m (3km) after **St Côme-du-Mont** turn right onto the D129, signposted **Hiesville**. At the first turning right (the D329 to Hiesville), stop on the verge just after the turning, staying on the D129. [101m, 163 km: 2h 50m from St. Malo, excluding the options in square brackets].   [2:50]   20:45

Now follow the **UTAH - NORTHBOUND MODULE** (page 15).   [2:05]   18:40
This links directly with the following modules:

STE MERE (page 11)	[3:10]	15:30
OMAHA - EASTBOUND (page 17)	[4:40]	10:50
BAYEUX (page 23)	[2:20]	8:30
GOLD - EASTBOUND (page 26)	[5:40]	2:50
PEGASUS (page 40)	[1:40]	1:10

From Pegasus Bridge carry on over the crossroads and over the bridge, following signs for **Caen** (5m, 8km) where you join the ring road.

[Here you may wish to visit Caen museum and/or city - this is NOT included in the timing. To do so, at the ring road turn right signposted **Cherbourg** then after 2m (3km) turn off at the sign for **Mémorial** (the name of the museum). Then follow further signs to **Mémorial** and park in the car park. Now follow the CAEN MODULE (page 53).]

To reach Argentan, at the **Caen** ring road initially follow the sign to the **A13**, but stay on the ring road until you turn off onto the the N158 to **Falaise** and **Argentan** (36m, 58km from where you joined the Caen ring road).

[As you will be following the direction of the TOTALISE - SOUTHBOUND MODULE (part of the Full Tour) when you reach the N158 roundabout, you may like to follow that module (see page 67) and also the FALAISE POCKET MODULE that leads on from it (page 72).]

[**41m, 66km: 1h 10m from Pegasus Bridge to Argentan, excluding the options in square brackets**].   [1:10]   0:00

FULL TOUR C

Total distance: 376m (605km)
Estimated time (hr:min): Travel 19:55 + Visits 15:45 = Total 35:40

Follow the Basic Tour (above) towards **St. Lo** (75m, 121km, from St Malo). Just before St. Lo, turn left at a roundabout onto the D972 signposted **Coutances** then right following signs to the D900 **Périers** road. Drive on through **Hébécrevon** and park in the lay-by just after the next crossroads (D77). **[80m, 129km: 2h 15m from St. Malo].**   [2:15] 33:25

Now follow the **COBRA MODULE** (page 46).   [1:40] 31:45
This links directly with the following modules:
UTAH - NORTHBOUND (page 15)	[2:05]	29:40
STE. MERE (page 11)	[3:10]	26:30
OMAHA - EASTBOUND (page 17)	[4:35]	21:55
GOLD - EASTBOUND (page 26)	[5:40]	16:15
PEGASUS (page 40)	[1:40]	14:35
MERVILLE (page 43)	[1:50]	12:45
GOODWOOD - SOUTHBOUND (page 61)	[1:10]	11:35
CAEN (page 53)	[2:35]	9:00
BAYEUX (page 23)	[2:15]	6:45
TILLY (page 48)	[0:55]	5:50
EPSOM (page 50)	[1:35]	4:15
TOTALISE - SOUTHBOUND (page 67)	[2:50]	1:25
FALAISE POCKET (page 72)	[1:10]	0:15

Drive through the village of **Tournai-sur-Dive** to **Villedieu-lès-Bailleul** and at the D916 turn left for **Argentan**. **[7m, 11km: 0h 15m].**   [0:15] 0:00

TOUR D: DETOUR GOING NORTH TO CHERBOURG

Begins: Argentan (35m, 56km, south of Caen on the N158).
Ends: Ferry terminal, Cherbourg.

BASIC TOUR D

		TIME(hr:min)	
		Module	To
Total distance:	183m (295km)	& link	finish
Estimated time ((hr:min) Travel 10:15 + Visits 12:00 = Total 22:15			

From **Argentan** take the N158, signposted **Caen**, to **Falaise**.
[From Falaise you will be following the direction of the
TOTALISE - NORTHBOUND MODULE (part of the Full Tour)
and you may like to read or even follow that module (see page
70). To do so, turn left in Falaise by the car park onto the **Vire**
road to **Musée Août 1944**.]

[After that you may wish to visit Caen museum and/or city. To
do so, follow the instructions below, but instead of turning off the
ring road for Ouistreham, carry on for another 2m (3km) and
turn off at the sign for **Mémorial** (the name of the museum).
Then follow further signs to **Mémorial** and park in the car park.
Now follow the CAEN MODULE (page 53).]

Continue to **Caen** where, at a roundabout, you turn right onto the
ring road, signposted **Cherbourg** (32m, 51km from Argentan).
After 2m (3km) turn right at the second interchange (coming very
soon after the first) onto the D513, signposted **Cherbourg**.   At
the second interchange, turn off towards **Ouistreham** (D515).
After 4m (6km) turn right to **Bénouville** and carry straight on
until you turn right onto the D514 signposted **Ranville**. **Pegasus
Bridge** is ahead of you.   Park just before the bridge.
[41m, 66km: 1h 10m from Argentan].   [1:10]   21:05

Now follow the **PEGASUS MODULE** (page 40).   [2:05]   19:00
This links directly with the following modules:

GOLD - WESTBOUND (page 34)	[5:45]	13:15
BAYEUX (page 23)	[2:20]	10:55
OMAHA - WESTBOUND (page 20)	[4:55]	6:00
UTAH - NORTHBOUND (page 15)	[2:05]	3:55
STE. MERE (page 11)	[2:35]	1:20

From the square in Ste. Mère Eglise return to the main street and turn left, then fork right to join the N13 for **Cherbourg** (24m, 39km). Having descended the hill into the town, look out for a signpost on the right to the **Fort du Roule** museum. If it is open (see Musée de la Guerre et de la Liberation on page 110), visit the museum - four minutes up a winding road - for as long as time allows [say 30 mins].

Return to the N13 and continue on to the ferry terminal (1m, 2km). There are many restaurants in the town. **[25m, 40km: 1h 20m from Ste. Mère Eglise].** [1:20] 0:00

FULL TOUR D

Total distance: 302m (486km)
Estimated time (hr:min): Travel 17:40 + Visits 16:15 = Total 33:55

At the end of the **Argentan** by-pass cross over the roundabout signposted **Dreux** and at the next roundabout turn left onto the D916 to **Trun** (8m, 13km). Here turn right onto the D13 St. **Lambert** road and, after the first hill, park on the verge when you can see the river valley ahead. **[9m, 15km: 0h 20m].** [0:20] 33:35

Now follow the **FALAISE POCKET MODULE** (page 72). [1:50] 31:45
This links directly with the following modules:

TOTALISE - NORTHBOUND (page 70)	[2:25]	29:20
GOODWOOD - NORTHBOUND (page 64)	[0:55]	28:25
CAEN (page 53)	[2:20]	26:05
PEGASUS (page 40)	[1:40]	24:25
MERVILLE (page 43)	[2:10]	22:15
GOLD - WESTBOUND (page 34)	[5:45]	16:30
BAYEUX (page 23)	[2:15]	14:15
TILLY (page 48)	[0:55]	13:20
EPSOM (page 50)	[2:10]	11:10
OMAHA - WESTBOUND (page 20)	[4:55]	6:15
UTAH - NORTHBOUND (page 15)	[2:05]	4:10
STE. MERE (page 11)	[2:35]	1:35

From Ste. Mère Eglise, follow the Basic Tour, but with the following variation if desired:-

A flying bomb (V1) launch site may be seen (but not visited as it is on private land) by turning off the N13 6m (10km) after **Valognes** onto the D56 signposted **St. Martin-le-G** then turn right towards **Le Theil**. Continue on that road for 2 miles (3km) and the site will be seen quite clearly on your left.

V1s, known as "doodle-bugs" or "buzz-bombs", killed over 5,000 people in England during June and July 1944, injured 35,000 and damaged 30,000 buildings.

Spend a few minutes there then return to the N13 the way you went.

[29m, 47km: 1h 35m to Cherbourg from Ste. Mère, via the V1 site].

[1:35]   0:00

Entanglements of Hitler's "Atlantic Wall" await the liberators one month before D-Day [IWM]

TOUR E: DETOUR GOING NORTH TO OUISTREHAM (CAEN)

Begins: Argentan (35m, 56km, south of Caen on the N158).
Ends: Ferry terminal, Ouistreham (9m, 14km, north of Caen).

[If you are making for the Channel Tunnel or ports from Le Havre to Calais, refer to page 105.]

BASIC TOUR E

		TIME(hr:min)	
		Module & link	To finish
Total distance:	207m (333km)		
Estimated time (hr:min): Travel 10:25 + Visits 11:30 = Total 21:55.			

From **Argentan** follow Basic Tour D (page 83) as far as **Pegasus Bridge.**   Park just before the bridge. **[41m, 66km: 1h 10m].**   [1:10] 20:45

Now follow the **PEGASUS MODULE** (page 40).   [1:40] 19:05
This links directly with the following modules:

	Module & link	To finish
GOLD - WESTBOUND (page 34)	[5:40]	13:25
OMAHA - WESTBOUND (page 20)	[4:55]	8:30
UTAH - NORTHBOUND (page 15)	[2:05]	6:25
STE. MERE (page 11)	[3:30]	2:55
BAYEUX (page 23)	[2:00]	0:55

From the Bayeux museum turn left to join the N13 to **Caen.**   On the Caen ring road follow signs for **Ouistreham** (D515). Follow signs to the ferry terminal.   There are many restaurants just before you reach the terminal. **[27m, 44km: 0h 55m].**   [0:55] 0:00

FULL TOUR E

Total distance: 294m (473km)
Estimated time (hr:min): Travel 17:20 + Visits 15:30 = Total 32:50

From the end of Argentan by-pass cross over the roundabout
signposted Dreux and at the next roundabout turn left onto the
D916 to Trun (8m, 13km). Here turn right onto the D13 St.
Lambert road and, after the first hill, park on the verge when
you can see the river valley ahead. [9m, 15km: 0h 20m].   [0:20] 32:30

Now follow the FALAISE POCKET MODULE (page 72).   [1:50] 30:40
This links directly with the following modules:

TOTALISE - NORTHBOUND (page 70)	[2:25]	28:15
GOODWOOD - NORTHBOUND (page 64)	[1:00]	27:15
PEGASUS (page 40)	[1:40]	25:35
MERVILLE (page 43)	[2:10]	23:25
GOLD - WESTBOUND (page 34)	[5:40]	17:45
OMAHA - WESTBOUND (page 20)	[4:55]	12:50
UTAH - NORTHBOUND (page 15)	[2:05]	10:45
STE MERE [see NOTE below] (page 11)	[3:30]	7:15
BAYEUX (page 23)	[2:15]	5:00
TILLY (page 48)	[0:55]	4:05
EPSOM (page 50)	[1:40]	2:25
CAEN (page 53)	[2:25]	0:00

At Ouistreham follow signs to the ferry terminal. There are
many restaurants just before you reach the terminal.   [0:00]   0:00

[NOTE: An opportunity is given after the Ste. Mère Module to
follow the COBRA MODULE.]

TOUR F: DETOUR GOING NORTH TO ST. MALO

Begins: Argentan (35m, 56km, south of Caen on the N158).
Ends: Ferry terminal, St. Malo.

BASIC TOUR F

		Module & link	To finish
		TIME(hr:min)	
Total distance:	263m (423km)		
Estimated time (hr:min):	Travel 12:25 + Visits 11:30 = Total 23:55		

From **Argentan** follow Basic Tour D (page 83) as far as **Pegasus Bridge.**   Park just before the bridge. [41m 66km: 1h 10m].   [1:10]   22:45

Now follow the **PEGASUS MODULE** (page 40).   [2:05]   20:40
This links directly with the following modules:

	Module & link	To finish
GOLD - WESTBOUND (page 34)	[5:45]	14:55
BAYEUX (page 23)	[2:20]	12:35
OMAHA - WESTBOUND (page 20)	[4:55]	7:40
UTAH - NORTHBOUND (page 15)	[2:05]	5:35
STE MERE (page 11)	[2:35]	3:00

[If you wish to follow the short COBRA MODULE (1 hour), follow the FULL TOUR at the end of the STE. MERE MODULE.]

From Ste. Mère Eglise square, return to the main street and turn left, following signs to **Carentan** (8m, 13km).   Carry on for 2m (3km) and turn right onto the N174 to **St. Lo** (20m, 32km). Following signs to **Le Mont St. Michel,** take the D999 to **Villedieu-lès-Poêles** (21m, 34km). [Poêles means pots and there are many shops in the centre of the town selling copperware - worth a quick visit.]   From there take the N175 around **Avranches** and follow signs to **St Malo.** [105m, 170km: 3h 00m from Ste Mère Eglise].   [3:00]   0:00

[If however you wish to see **Le Mont St. Michel,** turn right just after **Pontaubault** (4m, 7km after Avranches) onto the D275. Return to St Malo via the D976 to **Pontorson** then follow signs to **St Malo.**]

Total distance: 385m (620km)
Estimated time (hr:min): Travel 20:10 + Visits 15:45 = Total 35:55

At the end of the **Argentan** by-pass cross over the roundabout signposted **Dreux** and at the next roundabout turn left onto the D916 to **Trun** (8m, 13km). Here turn right onto the D13 **St. Lambert** road and, after the first hill, park on the verge when you can see the river valley ahead. **[9m, 15km: 0h 20m.]**   [0:20]   35:35

Now follow the **FALAISE POCKET MODULE** (page 72).   [1:50]   33:45
This links directly with:

TOTALISE - NORTHBOUND (page 70)	[2:25]	31:20
GOODWOOD - NORTHBOUND (page 64)	[0:55]	30:25
CAEN (page 53)	[2:20]	28:05
PEGASUS (page 40)	[1:40]	26:25
MERVILLE (page 43)	[2:10]	24:15
GOLD - WESTBOUND (page 34)	[5:50]	18:25
TILLY (page 48)	[0:55]	17:30
EPSOM (page 50)	[2:00]	15:30
BAYEUX (page 23)	[2:20]	13:10
OMAHA - WESTBOUND (page 20)	[4:55]	8:15
UTAH - NORTHBOUND (page 15)	[2:05]	6:10
STE MERE (page 11)	[3:25]	2:45
COBRA (page 46)	[0:45]	2:00

The last module left you on the D149 just east of La Chappelle-en-Juger. Turn right at the crossroads (no signpost) onto the D77 to **St. Gilles**. Follow the D77 straight across the D972 to **Canisy** and **Le Mesnil Herman** (8m, 13km).
Here turn right onto the D999 to **Villedieu-lès-Poêles** (15m, 24km). [Poêles means pots and there are many shops in the centre of the town selling copperware - worth a quick visit.]
From there take the N175 around **Avranches** and follow signs to **St. Malo**. **[76m, 122km: 2h 00m from La Chappelle-en-Juger].**   [2:00]   0:00

[If however you wish to see **Le Mont St. Michel**, turn right just after **Pontaubault** (4m, 7km after Avranches) onto the D275. Return to St Malo via the D976 to **Pontorson** then follow signs to **St. Malo.**]

TOUR G: CIRCULAR FROM CHERBOURG

Begins and ends: Ferry terminal, Cherbourg.

[If you are coming from the Channel Islands through Carteret, refer to page 105.]

BASIC TOUR G

		TIME(hr:min)	
		Module	To
Total distance:	218m (351km)	& link	finish
Estimated time (hr:min): Travel 11:05 + Visits 12:00 = Total 23:05			

From the ferry take the road opposite, following signs to **Caen**. After only 0.8m (1.3km), just after the last traffic lights and before the hill, is a turning left signposted (facing the opposite way!) **Fort du Roule**.   This museum is four minutes up a winding road and if it is open (see Musée de la Guerre et de la Libération on page 110) spend 30 minutes there.

Continue south on the N13, to **Ste. Mère Eglise**.   As you enter the town, just before the square, turn right signposted **La Poste** and, on the nearside, **Chef-du-Pont**.   Go under the N13, fork left on the D67 and, just after Chef-du-Pont (2.5m, 4km) as the river comes into view, park by the memorial on the right.
[28m, 45km: 1h 30m from the ferry.]   [1:30]   21:35

Now follow the **STE MERE MODULE** (page 11).   [2:35]   19:00
This links directly with the following modules:

UTAH - SOUTHBOUND (page 13)	[2:35]	16:25
OMAHA - EASTBOUND (page 17)	[4:35]	11:50
GOLD - EASTBOUND (page 26)	[5:40]	6:10
PEGASUS [see NOTE below] (page 40)	[2:30]	3:40
BAYEUX (page 23)	[2:00]	1:40

Turn right out of Bayeux Museum and at the roundabout take the N13 directly to the ferry terminal in **Cherbourg**.   There are many restaurants in the town. **[59m, 95km: 1h 40m].**   [1:40]   0:00

[NOTE: An opportunity is given after the Pegasus Module for a visit to Caen museum and/or city.]

FULL TOUR G

Total distance: 379m (610km)
Estimated time (hr:min): Travel 19:55 + Visits 16:15 = Total 36:10

From the ferry follow the Basic Tour above to **Chef-du-Pont**, but with the following variation:-
A flying bomb (V1) launch site may be seen (but not visited as it is on private land) by turning off the N13 (6m, 10km from the ferry terminal) at the sign to **Brix/St. Martin-le-G** then turn left, over the N13 signposted **Le Theil**.   Continue on that road for 2 miles (3km) and the site will be seen quite clearly on your left. *V1s, known as "doodle-bugs" or "buzz-bombs", killed over 5,000 people in England during June and July 1944, injured 35,000 and damaged 30,000 buildings.*
Spend a few minutes there then return to the N13 the way you went. **[32m, 52km: 1h 45m].**   [1:45] 34:25

Now follow the **STE MERE MODULE** (page 11).   [2:35] 31:50
This links directly with the following modules:

UTAH - SOUTHBOUND (page 13)	[2:35]	29:15
OMAHA - EASTBOUND (page 17)	[4:40]	24:35
BAYEUX (page 23)	[2:15]	22:20
TILLY (page 48)	[0:55]	21:25
EPSOM (page 50)	[1:40]	19:45
CAEN (page 53)	[2:25]	17:20
GOODWOOD - SOUTHBOUND (page 61)	[0:55]	16:25
TOTALISE - SOUTHBOUND (page 67)	[2:50]	13:35
FALAISE POCKET (page 72)	[2:25]	11:10
PEGASUS (page 40)	[1:40]	9:30
MERVILLE (page 43)	[2:10]	7:20
GOLD - WESTBOUND (page 34)	[5:25]	1:55

From **Arromanches**, take the D514 becoming the D516 to **Bayeux** where you turn right onto the N13 ring road.   At the roundabout (with the be-flagged General de Gaulle memorial in the centre), continue on the N13 directly to the ferry terminal in **Cherbourg**.   There are many restaurants in the town. **[68m, 109km : 1h 55m from Arromanches].**   [1:55]   0:00

TOUR H: CIRCULAR FROM OUISTREHAM (CAEN)

Begins and ends: Ferry terminal, Ouistreham (9m, 14km, north of Caen).

[If you are coming from the Channel Tunnel or ports from Le Havre to Calais, refer to page 105.]

BASIC TOUR H

		TIME(hr:min)	
		Module	To
Total distance:	168m (270km)	& link	finish

Estimated time (hr:min): Travel 9:25 + Visits 11:30 = Total 20:55

As you drive out of the ferry terminal at **Ouistreham,** turn very sharp right signposted **Plage** (beach) - **and don't forget to keep on the right!** As the road bears left you will see in a side street to your left a huge concrete tower built by the Germans to control the anti-aircraft defences for the port. Known as the flak tower, it now houses a museum.

Carry on until you reach a large building on the right, called **Queen Normandy.** This is a casino and on your left is the **No. 4 Commando Museum.**   Park on the right, opposite the museum. **[1m, 2km : 0h 5m].**   [0:05]   20:50

Now follow the **GOLD - WESTBOUND MODULE** (page 34).   [5:40]   15:10
This links directly with the following modules:

OMAHA - WESTBOUND (page 20)	[4:55]	10:15
UTAH - NORTHBOUND (page 15)	[2:05]	8:10
STE MERE (page 11)	[3:30]	4:40
BAYEUX (page 23)	[2:00]	2:40

From the **Bayeux** museum turn left to join the N13 to **Caen. [15m, 24km: 0h 25m].**   [0:25]   2:15

[Here you may wish to visit Caen museum and/or city - this is NOT included in the timing. To do so, at the Caen ring road, follow signs to **Mémorial** (the name of the museum) and park in the car park. Now follow the CAEN MODULE (page 53).]

On the Caen ring road, follow signs to **Ouistreham** (D515). 4m (6km) from the ring road turn right to **Bénouville** and carry straight on until you turn right onto the D514 signposted **Ranville. Pegasus Bridge** is ahead of you.   Park just before the bridge. **[9m, 14km: 0h 20m].**   [0:20]   1:55

Now follow the PEGASUS MODULE (page 40).   [1:40]   0:15

From Pegasus Bridge carry on over the crossroads and bear right
to **Ouistreham**. Follow signs to the ferry terminal.   There are
many restaurants just before you reach the terminal. **[4m, 7km:
0h 15m].**   [0:10]   0:00

FULL TOUR H

Total distance: 318m (512km)
Estimated time (hr:min): Travel 17:55 + Visits 15:30 = Total 33:25

Follow the Basic Tour (above) to the **No. 4 Commando
Museum. [1m, 2km: 0h 5m].**   [0:05] 33:20

Now follow the **GOLD - WESTBOUND MODULE** (page 34).   [5:40] 27:40
This links directly with the following modules:
OMAHA - WESTBOUND (page 20)	[4:55]	22:45
UTAH - NORTHBOUND (page 15)	[2:05]	20:40
STE MERE [see NOTE below] (page 11)	[3:30]	17:10
BAYEUX (page 23)	[2:15]	14:55
TILLY (page 48)	[0:55]	14:00
EPSOM (page 50)	[1:40]	12:20
CAEN (page 53)	[2:25]	9:55
GOODWOOD - SOUTHBOUND (page 61)	[0:55]	9:00
TOTALISE - SOUTHBOUND (page 67)	[2:50]	6:10
FALAISE POCKET (page 72)	[2:25]	3:45
PEGASUS (page 40)	[1:40]	2:05
MERVILLE (page 43)	[1:40]	0:25

Continue over the crossroads then immediately fork right onto the
D244 through **Ranville** to **Pegasus Bridge**. Carry on over the
crossroads and bear right to **Ouistreham**. Follow signs to the
ferry terminal. There are many restaurants just before you reach
the terminal. **[8m, 13km: 0h 25m].**   [0:25]   0:00

[NOTE: An opportunity is given after the Ste. Mère Module to
follow the COBRA MODULE.]

TOUR I: CIRCULAR TOUR FROM ST. MALO

Begins and ends: Ferry terminal, St. Malo.

[Visits to the town of St. Malo and to Le Mont St. Michel are recommended but are best left to the end of the tour, if you have time.   They are NOT included in the timing.]

BASIC TOUR I

TIME(hr:min)

Total distance: 335m (539km)
Estimated time (hr:min): Travel 13:55 + Visits 11:30 = Total 25:25

Module   To
& link   finish

From **St. Malo** take the D4 to **Dol de Bretagne** then the N176/175 towards **Avranches** (40m, 65km).

[If you do wish to visit **Le Mont St Michel** at this point turn left at **Pontorson** (27m, 43km, from St Malo) and continue for 6 miles (9km).   You can rejoin the tour by turning left from Le Mont onto the D275 for **Avranches**.   This side-trip is NOT included in the timing.]

Go around the **Avranches** by-pass to **Villedieu-les-Poêles** (14m, 22km).   [Poêles means pots and there are many shops in the centre of the town selling copperware - worth a quick visit.] From here follow signs to **St. Lo** (21m, 34km).

[If you wish to follow the short COBRA MODULE, follow the FULL TOUR at this point.]

Following signs to **Cherbourg** from **St. Lo** take the N174/N13 to **Carentan** (20m, 32km).   Once past Carentan, 2m (3km) after **St Côme-du-Mont** turn right onto the D129, signposted **Hiesville**.   At the first turning right (the D329 to Hiesville), stop on the verge just after the turning, staying on the D129. **[101m, 163km: 2h 50m from St. Malo].**   [2:50]   22:35

Now follow the **UTAH - NORTHBOUND MODULE** (page 15).   [2:05]   20:30
This links directly with the following modules:
STE MERE (page 11)   [3:10]   17:20
OMAHA - EASTBOUND (page 17)   [4:40]   12:40
BAYEUX (page 23)   [2:20]   10:20
GOLD - EASTBOUND (page 26)   [5:40]   4:40
PEGASUS (page 40)   [1:40]   3:00

From Pegasus Bridge carry on over the crossroads and over the
bridge, following signs for **Caen** to the ring road (5m, 8km).

[Here you may wish to visit Caen museum and/or city - this is
NOT included in the timing. To do so, at the ring road turn right
signposted **Cherbourg** then after 2m (3km) turn off at the sign
for **Mémorial** (the name of the museum). Then follow further
signs to **Mémorial** and park in the car park. Now follow the
CAEN MODULE (page 53).]

At the Caen ring road, initially follow signs to **Cherbourg** and
then aim for the N175 signposted **Le Mt St. Michel** to
Avranches and **St Malo**. [114m, 183km: 3h 00m from
Pegasus].   [3:00]   0:00

[If however you wish to see **Le Mont St. Michel**, turn right just
after **Pontaubault** (4m, 7km after Avranches) onto the D275.
Return to St. Malo via the D976 to **Pontorson** then follow signs
to **St. Malo**.]

FULL TOUR I

Total distance: 487m (784km)

Estimated time (hr:min): Travel 24:20 + Visits 15:45 = Total 40:05

	Module & link	To finish

Follow the Basic Tour (above) towards **St. Lo** (75m, 121km, from St Malo). Just before St. Lo, turn left at a roundabout onto the D972 signposted **Coutances** then right following signs to the D900 **Périers** road. Drive on through **Hébécrevon** and park in the lay-by just after the next crossroads (D77). **[81m, 131km: 2h 15m from St. Malo.]**   [2:15] 37:50

Now follow the **COBRA MODULE** (page 46).   [1:40] 36:10
This links directly with the following modules:

	Module & link	To finish
UTAH - NORTHBOUND (page 15)	[2:05]	34:05
STE MERE (page 11)	[3:10]	30:55
OMAHA - EASTBOUND (page 17)	[4:35]	26:20
GOLD - EASTBOUND (page 26)	[5:40]	20:40
PEGASUS (page 40)	[1:40]	19:00
MERVILLE (page 43)	[1:50]	17:10
GOODWOOD - SOUTHBOUND (page 61)	[1:10]	16:00
CAEN (page 53)	[2:35]	13:25
BAYEUX (page 23)	[2:15]	11:10
TILLY (page 48)	[0:55]	10:15
EPSOM (page 50)	[1:35]	8:40
TOTALISE - SOUTHBOUND (page 67)	[2:50]	5:50
FALAISE POCKET (page 72)	[1:10]	4:40

Drive through the village of Tournai-sur-Dive to **Villedieu-lès-Bailleul** and at the D916 turn left for **Argentan** (7m, 11km). From **Argentan** take the D924 westwards to **Ecouché** and **Flers** (27m, 43km) - this follows the route (in the opposite direction) taken by the German army fleeing the American advance. From Flers take the D25 signposted **Mortain**. After it becomes the D157, and just after **Ger** (13m, 21km from Flers), stop as you are about to descend the hill.

This is the area where the Germans carried out their final counter-attack of the Normandy campaign. Mortain is seven miles ahead and, in the early hours of 7th August, from there they pressed seven miles into the American lines in a desperate bid to stop the U.S. advance. Without any air cover of their own, they were attacked at noon by U.S. Thunderbolts and R.A.F rocket-firing Typhoons and the German columns crowding the roads ahead of you were subjected to a pounding they had never experienced before. In spite of this, Hitler insisted they should stay and fight, but when the Americans came up from your left and hit the Germans at Ger behind you, they decided it was time to go and the disorderly retreat to the Seine began.

Carry on to **Mortain,** then take the D977 to **St. Hilaire-du-Harcouët** (9m, 14km) and **Pontaubault** (south of Avranches) (12m, 20km). From here you can follow signs to **Le Mont St. Michel** or to **St. Malo,** as desired. **[117m, 188km: 4h 40m to St. Malo from Tournai].**   [4:40]   0:00

Villagers washing Canadian soldiers' clothes in Reviers [IWM]
- see pages 31 or 37

TOUR J: ONE-WAY FROM CHERBOURG TO OUISTREHAM (CAEN)

Begins: Ferry terminal, Cherbourg.
Ends: Ferry terminal, Ouistreham (9m, 14km, north of Caen).

[If you are making for Le Havre, refer to page 105.]

BASIC TOUR J

Total distance: 145m (233km)
Estimated time (hr:min): Travel 9:15 + Visits 12:00 = Total 21:15

	TIME(hr:min)	
	Module & link	To finish

From the ferry take the road opposite, following signs to **Caen**. After only 0.8m (1.3km), just after the last traffic lights and before the hill, there is a turning left signposted (facing the opposite way!) **Fort du Roule**. This museum is four minutes up a winding road and if it is open (see Musée de la Guerre et de la Libération on page 110) spend 30 minutes there.

Continue south on the N13, to **Ste Mère Eglise**. As you enter the town, just before the square, turn right signposted **La Poste** and, on the nearside, **Chef-du-Pont**. Go under the N13, fork left on the D67 and, just after Chef-du-Pont (2.5m, 4km) as the river comes into view, park by the memorial on the right. **[28m, 45km: 1h 30m from the ferry].** [1:30] 19:45

Now follow the **STE MERE MODULE** (page 11). [2:35] 17:10
This links directly with the following modules:

UTAH - SOUTHBOUND (page 13)	[2:35]	14:35
OMAHA - EASTBOUND (page 17)	[4:40]	9:55
BAYEUX (page 23)	[2:20]	7:35
GOLD - EASTBOUND (page 26)	[5:40]	1:55
PEGASUS [see NOTE below] (page 40)	[1:40]	0:15

From Pegasus Bridge carry on over the crossroads and bear right to **Ouistreham**. Follow signs to the ferry terminal. There are many restaurants just before you reach the terminal. **[4m, 7km: 0h 15m].** [0:15] 0:00

[NOTE: An opportunity is given after the Pegasus Module for a visit to Caen museum and/or city.]

FULL TOUR J

TIME(hr:min)

Total distance: 331m (533km)

Estimated time (hr:min): Travel 18:55 + Visits 16:15 = Total 35:10

	Module & link	To finish

From the ferry follow the Basic Tour above to **Chef-du-Pont**, but with the following variation:-

A flying bomb (V1) launch site may be seen (but not visited as it is on private land) by turning off the N13 (6m, 10km from the ferry terminal) at the sign to **Brix/St. Martin-le-G** then turn left, over the N13 signposted **Le Theil**. Continue on that road for 2 miles (3km) and the site will be seen quite clearly on your left. *V1s, known as "doodle-bugs" or "buzz-bombs", killed over 5,000 people in England during June and July 1944, injured 35,000 and damaged 30,000 buildings.*

Spend a few minutes there then return to the N13 the way you went. **[32m, 52km: 1h 45]**.   [1:45]   33:25

Now follow the **STE MERE MODULE** (page 11).   [2:35]   30:50

This links directly with the following modules:

UTAH - SOUTHBOUND (page 13)	[2:35]	28:15
OMAHA - EASTBOUND (page 17)	[4:40]	23:35
BAYEUX (page 23)	[2:15]	21:20
TILLY (page 48)	[0:55]	20:25
EPSOM (page 50)	[1:40]	18:45
CAEN (page 53)	[2:25]	16:20
GOODWOOD - SOUTHBOUND (page 61)	[0:55]	15:25
TOTALISE - SOUTHBOUND (page 67)	[2:50]	12:35
FALAISE POCKET (page 72)	[3:10]	9:25
GOLD - EASTBOUND (page 26)	[5:40]	3:45
PEGASUS (page 40)	[1:40]	2:05
MERVILLE (page 43)	[1:40]	0:25

Continue over the crossroads then immediately fork right onto the D244 through **Ranville** to **Pegasus Bridge**. Carry on over the crossroads and bear right to **Ouistreham**. Follow signs to the ferry terminal. There are many restaurants just before you reach the terminal. **[8m, 13km: 0h 25m]**.   [0:25]   0:00

TOUR K: ONE-WAY FROM OUISTREHAM (CAEN) TO ST. MALO

Begins: Ferry terminal, Ouistreham (9m, 14km, north of Caen).
Ends: Ferry terminal, St. Malo.

[If you are coming from the Channel Tunnel or ports from Le Havre to Calais, refer to page 105.]

BASIC TOUR K

		TIME(hr:min)	
		Module & link	To finish
Total distance:	225m (362km)		
Estimated time (hr:min):	Travel 11:20 + Visits 11:30 = Total 22:50		

Drive straight out of the ferry terminal following signs firstly to **Autres Directions** and then **Caen**. After 3m (5km) turn off onto the D514 ·**Bénouville** and **Ranville** (NOT the D35 Zone d'Activités de Bénouville) and keep straight on to **Pegasus Bridge**. Park just before the bridge. [4m, 7km: 0h 15m].   [0:15]   22:35

Now follow the **PEGASUS MODULE** (page 40)   [2:05]   20:30

[NOTE: An opportunity is given after the Pegasus Module for a visit to Caen museum and/or city.]

This links directly with the following modules:

GOLD - WESTBOUND (page 34)	[5:45]	14:45
BAYEUX (page 23)	[2:20]	12:25
OMAHA - WESTBOUND (page 20)	[4:55]	7:30
UTAH - NORTHBOUND (page 15)	[2:05]	5:25
STE MERE (page 11)	[2:35]	2:50

[If you wish to follow the short COBRA MODULE (1 hour), follow FULL F at the end of the STE. MERE MODULE.]

From Ste. Mère Eglise square, return to the main street and turn left, following signs to **Carentan** (8m, 13km). Carry on for 2m (3km) and turn right onto the N174 to **St. Lo** (20m, 32km). Following signs to **Le Mont St. Michel**, take the D999 to **Villedieu-lès-Poêles** (21m, 34km). [Poêles means pots and there are many shops in the centre of the town selling copperware - worth a quick visit.] From there take the N175 around

Avranches and follow signs to St Malo. [104m, 167km: 2h 50m from Ste Mère Eglise].   [2:50]   0:00

[If however you wish to see **Le Mont St. Michel,** turn right just after **Pontaubault** (4m, 7km after Avranches) onto the D275. Return to St Malo via the D976 to **Pontorson** then follow signs to **St Malo.**]

FULL TOUR K

Total distance: 395m (636km)
Estimated time (hr:min): Travel 21:35 + Visits 15:30 = Total 37:05

From the ferry follow the Basic Tour (above) to **Pegasus Bridge.** Park just before the bridge. **[4m, 7km: 0h 15m].**   [0:15]   36:50

Now follow the **PEGASUS MODULE** (page 40).   [1:40]   35:10
This links directly with the following modules:

MERVILLE (page 43)	[2:10]	33:00
GOLD - WESTBOUND (page 34)	[5:40]	27:20
OMAHA - WESTBOUND (page 20)	[4:55]	22:25
UTAH - NORTHBOUND (page 15)	[2:05]	20:20
STE MERE [see NOTE below] (page 11)	[3:30]	16:50
BAYEUX (page 23)	[2:15]	14:35
TILLY (page 48)	[0:55]	13:40
EPSOM (page 50)	[1:40]	12:00
CAEN (page 53)	[2:25]	9:35
GOODWOOD - SOUTHBOUND (page 61)	[0:55]	8:40
TOTALISE - SOUTHBOUND (page 67)	[2:50]	5:50
FALAISE POCKET (page 72)	[1:10]	4:40

Drive through the village of **Tournai-sur-Dive** to **Villedieu-lès-Bailleul** and at the D916 turn left for **Argentan** (7m, 11km).

From **Argentan** follow the Full Tour of TOUR I: CIRCULAR TOUR FROM ST. MALO (page 96). **[117m, 188km: 4h 40m to St. Malo from Tournai].**   [4:40]   0:00

[NOTE: An opportunity is given after the St. Mère Module to follow the COBRA MODULE.]

TOUR L: ONE-WAY FROM CHERBOURG TO ST. MALO

Begins: Ferry terminal, Cherbourg.
Ends: Ferry terminal, St. Malo.

[If you are coming from the Channel Islands through Carteret, refer to page 105.]

BASIC TOUR L

		TIME(hr:min)	
		Module	To
Total distance:	255m (410km)	& link	finish
Estimated time (hr:min): Travel 12:00 + Visits 12:00 = Total 24:00			

From the ferry take the road opposite, following signs to **Caen**.
After only 0.8m (1.3km), just after the last traffic lights and
before the hill, there is a turning left signposted (facing the
opposite way!) **Fort du Roule**.   This museum is four minutes up
a winding road and if it is open (see Musée de la Guerre et de la
Libération on page 110) spend 30 minutes there.
Continue south on the N13, to **Ste. Mère Eglise**.   As you enter
the town, just before the square, turn right signposted **La Poste**
and, on the nearside, **Chef-du-Pont**.   Go under the N13, fork
left on the D67 and, just after Chef-du-Pont (2.5m, 4km) as the
river comes into view, park by the memorial on the right.
[28m, 45km: 1h 30m from the ferry].   [1:30] 22:30

Now follow the **STE. MERE MODULE** (page 11).   [2:35] 19:55
This links directly with the following modules:

UTAH - SOUTHBOUND (page 13)	[2:35]	17:20
OMAHA - EASTBOUND (page 17)	[4:40]	12:40
BAYEUX (page 23)	[2:20]	10:20
GOLD - EASTBOUND (page 26)	[5:40]	4:40
PEGASUS (page 40)	[1:40]	3:00

From Pegasus Bridge carry on over the crossroads and over the
bridge, following signs for **Caen** to the ring road (5m, 8km).

[The rest of the Basic Tour is simply the journey to St. Malo,
including if you wish, visits to Le Mont St. Michel and St. Malo
itself.   Before you leave Caen you may like to visit the museum
and/or city - this is NOT included in the timing.   To do so, at the
ring road turn right signposted **Cherbourg** then after 2m (3km)
turn off at the sign for **Mémorial** (the name of the museum)

and follow further signs for **Mémorial**.   Park in the car park.
Now follow the CAEN MODULE (page 53).]

At the Caen ring road, initially follow signs for **Cherbourg** and
then aim for the N175 signposted **Le Mt. St. Michel**.   On the
way the road by-passes **Villedieu-les-Poêles**. [Poêles means pots
and there are many shops in the centre of the town which are
worth a quick visit].   Continue on around **Avranches**
(65m, 104km) to **St. Malo** (40m, 65km). **[114m, 183km:
3h 00m from Pegasus]**.   [3:00]   0:00

[To visit **Le Mont St. Michel** turn right just after **Pontaubault**
(4m, 7km, after Avranches) onto the D275 (9m, 15km).   Return
to **St Malo** via the D976 to **Pontorson**.]

FULL TOUR L

Total distance: 408m (657km)
Estimated time (hr:min): Travel 21:50 + Visits 16:15 = Total 38:05

From the ferry follow the Basic Tour above to **Chef-du-Pont**, but
with the following variation:-
A flying bomb (V1) launch site may be seen (but not visited as
it is on private land) by turning off the N13 (6m,10km, from the
ferry terminal) at the sign to **Brix/St. Martin-le-G** then turn left,
over the N13 signposted **Le Theil**.   Continue on that road for
2 miles (3km) and the site will be seen quite clearly on your left.
*V1s, known as "doodle-bugs" or "buzz-bombs", killed over 5,000
people in England during June and July 1944, injured 35,000 and
damaged 30,000 buildings.*
Spend a few minutes there then return to the N13 the way you
went. **[32m, 52km: 1h 45m]**.   [1:45] 36:20

Now follow the **STE MERE MODULE** (page 11).   [2:35]   33:45
This links directly with the following modules:

UTAH - SOUTHBOUND (page 13)	[2:35]	31:10
OMAHA - EASTBOUND (page 17)	[4:35]	26:35
BAYEUX (page 23)	[2:15]	24:20
TILLY (page 48)	[0:55]	23:25
EPSOM (page 50)	[1:40]	21:45
CAEN (page 53)	[2:25]	19:20
GOLD - EASTBOUND (page 26)	[5:40]	13:40
PEGASUS (page 40)	[1:40]	12:00
MERVILLE (page 43)	[2:25]	9:35
GOODWOOD - SOUTHBOUND (page 61)	[0:55]	8:40
TOTALISE - SOUTHBOUND (page 67)	[2:50]	5:50
FALAISE POCKET (page 72)	[1:10]	4:40

Drive through the village of **Tournai-sur-Dive** to **Villedieu-lès-
Bailleul** and at the D916 turn left for **Argentan** (7m, 11km).

Now return to **St Malo** by following the end of the Full Tour of
TOUR I: CIRCULAR TOUR FROM ST. MALO (page 96).
[117m, 188km: 4h 40m to St. Malo from Tournai].   [4:40]   0:00

CONNECTIONS WITH CHANNEL ISLANDS, CHANNEL TUNNEL AND PORTS FROM LE HAVRE TO CALAIS

CHANNEL ISLANDS

Visitors from the Channel Islands taking a detour from their route to a holiday elsewhere should take Tours C or F via St. Malo. For a circular tour with your own car, take Tour I from St. Malo. If you wish to drive with a hire car, you can hire a car through Avis, Europcar or Hertz for the circular tour from St Malo or through Emeraude Lines for a circular trip from Carteret (see Appendix page 108).

CONNECTIONS TO TOUR G. If you go to Carteret you will join circular Tour G (which starts at Cherbourg) by taking the D902 to **Valognes** where you turn right onto the N13 to **Ste. Mère Eglise** (29m, 46km). You then carry on with Tour G (page 90). On your return, leave the N13 Cherbourg road at **Carentan** (26m, 42km, from Bayeux) turning left onto the D903 through **St. Jores** and **La Haye-du-Puits** to **Barneville-Carteret** (29m, 46km, from Carentan). The "time to finish" readings on the tour page are almost the same for Carteret as for Cherbourg.

CHANNEL TUNNEL AND PORTS FROM LE HAVRE TO CALAIS

If you are on your way to a holiday elsewhere in France and wish to take one of the **detours,** make for **Ouistreham** and follow Tour B (or, if you are going on the holiday first, make for **Argentan** and follow Tour E). If you wish to do a circular tour and are not using the direct Brittany Ferry route from Portsmouth, then make for **Ouistreham** and take Tour H.

TO REACH OUISTREHAM

From **Le Havre,** aim for the **A15** to **Pont de Tancarville** bridge across the River Seine 20m (32km) east of Le Havre. After the bridge, turn off onto the N178 which leads you to the A13 Autoroute de Normandie to **Caen.** At the Caen ring road the A13 becomes the N413 and after 2m (3km) turn off onto the D515 towards **Ouistreham** (77m, 124km from Le Havre). Those following Tour B need not go all the way there, but should turn right 4m (7km) from the Caen ring road at the signpost to **Bénouville** then at a crossroads turn right onto the D514 signposted **Ranville. Pegasus Bridge** is just ahead of you. Park just before the bridge.

From the **Channel Tunnel** and from **Dieppe and all other ports to the east,** you should make for **Rouen** (128m, 206km, from Calais), to the south of which you pick up the A13 Autoroute de Normandie and make for **Caen** and **Ouistreham** as described above. Ouistreham is 83m (133km) from Rouen.

TO RETURN EASTWARDS AFTER BASIC E OR FULL E

On the Caen ring road, follow signs to the **A13** Autoroute de Normandie.

TO RETURN EASTWARDS AFTER BASIC H OR J

From Pegasus Bridge carry on over the crossroads and over the bridge, following signs for **Caen**. At the ring road (4m, 7km) turn off to join the **A13** Autoroute de Normandie. Le Havre is 73m (117km) from Pegasus and can be reached in well under two hours driving at the speed limit. This includes stopping at three toll stations (péage) - the first two will take your credit card, but the third only takes cash.

TO RETURN EASTWARDS AFTER FULL H OR J

If you have plenty of time, complete the tour and at Pegasus Bridge follow "Basic H or J" above. If you are in a hurry you could break off near the end of the Merville module when it is at its most easterly point, Varaville. Take the D27 over the River Dives and turn right at the crossroads to join the **A13**. Turn left for Le Havre or Rouen.

APPENDIX

FERRIES

You should obtain the latest ferry timetables and short-break brochures from the appropriate ferry operators or a travel agent (see Accommodation on page 108). Sailing times vary considerably, depending on the day of the week and the time of year.

Brittany Ferries (0705 827701)
The Brittany Centre,
Wharf Road,
Portsmouth PO2 8RU.
   Portsmouth to Caen (Ouistreham) and St. Malo
   Poole to Cherbourg

P & O European Ferries (0705 772000)
Peninsular House,
Wharf Road,
Portsmouth PO2 8TA.
   Portsmouth to Cherbourg and Le Havre

Stena Sealink Line (0703 233973)
Charter House,
Park Street,
Ashford, Kent TN24 8EX.
   Southampton to Cherbourg

Emeraude Lines
5 Esplanade,
Saint-Helier, Jersey.
   Car ferry to St. Malo
     from Jersey (534 66566)
     from Guernsey (481 711414)
   Passenger ferry to Carteret (they arrange car hire)
     from Jersey (534 56792)
   Passenger ferry to St. Malo (they arrange car hire)
     from Jersey (534 66566)
     from Guernsey (481 711414)

Condor (0305-761551)
Weymouth Quay,
Dorset DT4 8DX.
   Passenger ferry to St. Malo
     from Jersey (534 76300)
     from Guernsey (481 726121)

CAR HIRE

If you wish to arrange for a car to meet you at the ferry, it would be best to arrange it on the London phone number. The local numbers are given here in case of difficulty.

Avis (London 081-848-8733, Caen 31 87 73 80, Cherbourg 33 43 16 00, Le Havre 35 53 17 20, St. Malo 99 81 73 24).

Europcar (London 081-950-5050, Caen 31 84 57 38, Cherbourg 33 44 53 85, Le Havre 35 25 21 95, St. Malo 99 56 75 17).

Hertz (London 081-679-1799, Caen 31 84 64 50, Cherbourg 33 20 48 11, Le Havre 35 53 20 34, St. Malo 99 56 31 61).

At Carteret - book through Emeraude Lines (Jersey (534) 56792, Guernsey (481) 711414, Carteret 33 52 61 39).

TOURIST INFORMATION OFFICES

(Offices de Tourisme or Syndicats d'Initiative - follow "i" signs)
Bayeux - 1 Rue des Cuisiniers, 14403 Bayeux CEDEX (Tel: 31 92 16 26)
Caen - Place Saint-Pierre, 14000 Caen (Tel: 31 86 27 65)

These offices will send you a town map and details of places of interest, local events and accommodation (see below). There are tourist offices in many other towns.

ACCOMMODATION

There is ample accommodation in Normandy including hotels, homes offering bed and breakfast (chambres d'hôtes), caravan sites and camp sites - far too many to list here. You may obtain full details by writing to or telephoning either of the tourist offices above (in English if you wish). You should book well in advance if possible as this is a very popular holiday area.

The simplest way is to book a "short break" with one of the ferry companies, which includes hotel or chambres d'hôte accommodation. If you plan your tour in advance, you will be able to decide approximately where you will be each evening. If you decide to stay at a hotel, then either Bayeux or Caen will be quite suitable as it does not take very long to reach either from anywhere in the tour area. At the appropriate time, with help from a map, you break off the tour and return to it next morning. It takes only 45 minutes to drive from the centre of Bayeux to the centre of Caen and about the same from St. Mère Eglise to Bayeux.

ADDITIONAL READING

There are many books on the subject of D-Day available in public libraries and in bookshops. The following were used in compiling this book:

"*Six Armies in Normandy*" John Keegan 1982 (Jonathan Cape) and 1983 (Penguin Books) *

"*The Visitor's Guide to the Normandy Landing Beaches, Memorials and Museums*" Tonie and Valmai Holt 1989 (Moorland Publishing Co.) **

"*Holts' Battlefield Guides (Normandy-Overlord)*" Tonie and Valmai Holt 1988 (T & V Holt Associates)

"*Normandy 1944*" Jean Pierre Benamou 1982 (Heimdal, Bayeux) ***

"*The Struggle for Europe*" Chester Wilmot 1952 (Collins)

*   This book, by the Defence Editor of the Daily Telegraph, will make excellent reading as a follow-up to your tour, as its descriptions will be made even more vivid by your own memories.   Also available from Telegraph Books (tel: 071-537-2207).

**   This guide is highly recommended for visitors interested in more military detail and in lively accounts of the battle by some of those taking part.

*** Dr. Benamou is the curator of the Bayeux Battle of Normandy museum where the book is on sale. It contains a wealth of photographs.

Shell damaged World War I memorial in Longèvres [IWM] - see page 48

OPENING TIMES OF MUSEUMS AND OTHER SITES
All times are subject to alteration

ENGLAND

Portsmouth D-Day Museum (0705-827261)
Clarence Esplanade
Includes Overlord Embroidery
    Daily   1030-1730 (except 24-26 Dec)

Southwick House (0705-210522 Ext. 4221)
Portsmouth
General Eisenhower's headquarters - includes D-Day wall map
    Mon-Fri   0900-1200, 1400-1700
By appointment only

FRANCE (listed from west to east)

Musée de la Guerre et de la Libération (33 20 14 12)
Fort du Roule, Cherbourg
    Nov-Mar   0930-1200,1400-1730 (Daily except Tue)
    Apr-Oct   0900-1200,1400-1800 (Daily)

U.S. Airborne Museum & C47 Museum (33 41 41 35)
Ste Mère Eglise
    1 Feb-31 May, 15 Sep-14 Nov   0900-1200, 1400-1900
    1 Jun-14 Sep   0900-1900
    16-31 Jan, 15 Nov-14 Dec   1000-1200/1400 (Sat/Sun only)
    15 Dec-15 Jan   Closed

Musée du Debarquement (33 71 53 35 or 33 71 58 00)
Utah Beach
    Easter-1 Nov   0900-1200, 1400-1900
    1 Nov-31 Dec, 1 Feb-Easter   1000-1200, 1400-1600
    January   Closed

American National Cemetery and Memorial (31 22 40 62)
St Laurent
    Summer - weekdays   0900-1800
              - weekends/holidays 1000-1800
    Winter   - weekdays   0900-1700
              - weekends/holidays 1000-1700

Musée Mémorial de la Battaille de Normandie (31 92 93 41)
Boulevard Fabian Ware, Bayeux (opposite the British Military Cemetery)
    Jun - Aug   0900-1900
    Mar - May, Sep - Oct   0930-1230, 1400-1830
    Nov - Feb (Sat/Sun only)   1000-1230, 1400-1800

OPENING TIMES OF MUSEUMS AND OTHER SITES
(continued)

Bayeux Tapestry (Tapisserie de la Reine Mathilde) (31 92 05 48)
Centre Guillaume le Conquérant,
Rue de Nesmond, Bayeux
  Daily except Jan 1 & Dec 25 and Jan 2 & Dec 26 (mornings)

Musée du Débarquement (Landings Museum) (31 22 34 31)
Arromanches
Daily	0900-1130, 1400-1730
Jun - Aug	0900-1830 (Mon opens 1000)
Jan 1 - 22	Closed .

No. 4 Commando Museum (31 96 36 10)
Ouistreham (opposite the Casino)
Jun - Sep, Easter	0900-1800
Easter - May, Oct	0930-1730
Nov - Easter	Closed

Atlantic Wall Great Bunker Museum (31 97 28 69)
Avénue du 6 juin, Ouistreham
Apr - Mid Nov	0900-1900
Mid Nov - Mar (weekends)	1000-1200, 1400-1800

Musée des Troupes Aéroportées Britanniques (31 44 62 54)
Pegasus Bridge, Bénouville
Mid Mar - Jun 30	0930-1230, 1400-1800 (1900 in June)
Jul 1 - Aug 31	0900-1900
Sep 1 - Mid Oct	0930-1230, 1400-1800
Mid Oct - Mid Mar	Closed

Merville Battery Museum (31 24 21 83)
Easter - Sep 15	1030-1230, 1430-1830 (Closed Tue)
Sep 16 - Easter	Closed

Mémorial (un musée pour la paix - a museum for peace) (31 06 06 44)
Caen
Daily	0900-1900
Jul 11 - Aug 31	0900-2100
Jan 1-15, Mar 21, Dec 25	Closed

Musée Août 1944 (August 1944 Museum) (31 90 37 19)
Falaise
Mar - May	1400 - 1800 Closed Mon/Tue
Jun - Aug	1400 - 1800 Daily
Sep - Nov	1400 - 1800 Closed Mon/Tue
Dec - Feb	Closed

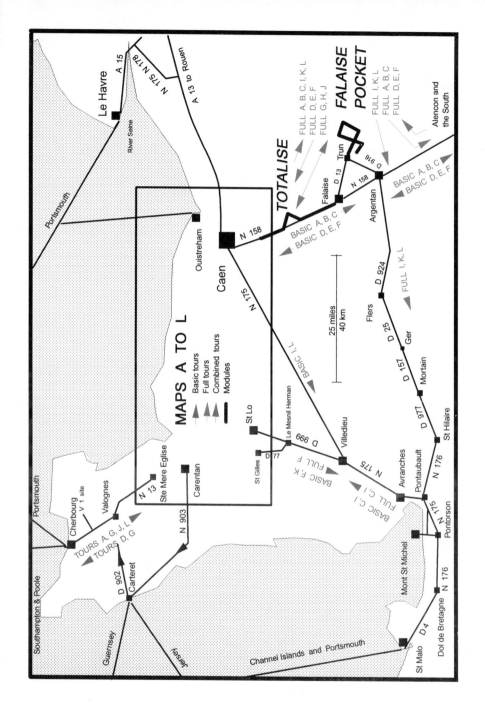

MAPS A TO L

Basic tours
Full tours
Combined tours
Modules

FALAISE POCKET

TOTALISE

FULL A, B, C, I, K, L
FULL D, E, F
FULL G, H, J

FULL I, K, L
FULL A, B, C
FULL D, E, F

Alençon and the South

BASIC A, B, C
BASIC D, E, F

BASIC A, B, C
BASIC D, E, F

FULL I, K, L

BASIC I, L
FULL C, I

BASIC C, I
FULL F, K

TOURS A, G, J, L
TOURS D, G

25 miles
40 km

Le Havre
A 15
N 175 N 178
A 13 to Rouen
River Seine
Portsmouth
Ouistreham
Caen
N 158
N 175
Falaise
D 13
Trun
D 916
N 158
Argentan
D 924
Flers
D 25
Ger
D 157
Mortain
D 977
St Hilaire
N 176
Avranches
Pontaubault
Pontorson
N 175
Mont St Michel
St Malo
D 4
Dol de Bretagne
N 176
Channel Islands and Portsmouth
St Lo
Le Mesnil Herman
D 999
St Gilles
D 77
Villedieu
N 175
Portsmouth
Cherbourg
V 1 site
Valognes
N 13
Ste Mere Eglise
Carentan
N 903
D 902
Carteret
Guernsey
Jersey
Southampton & Poole

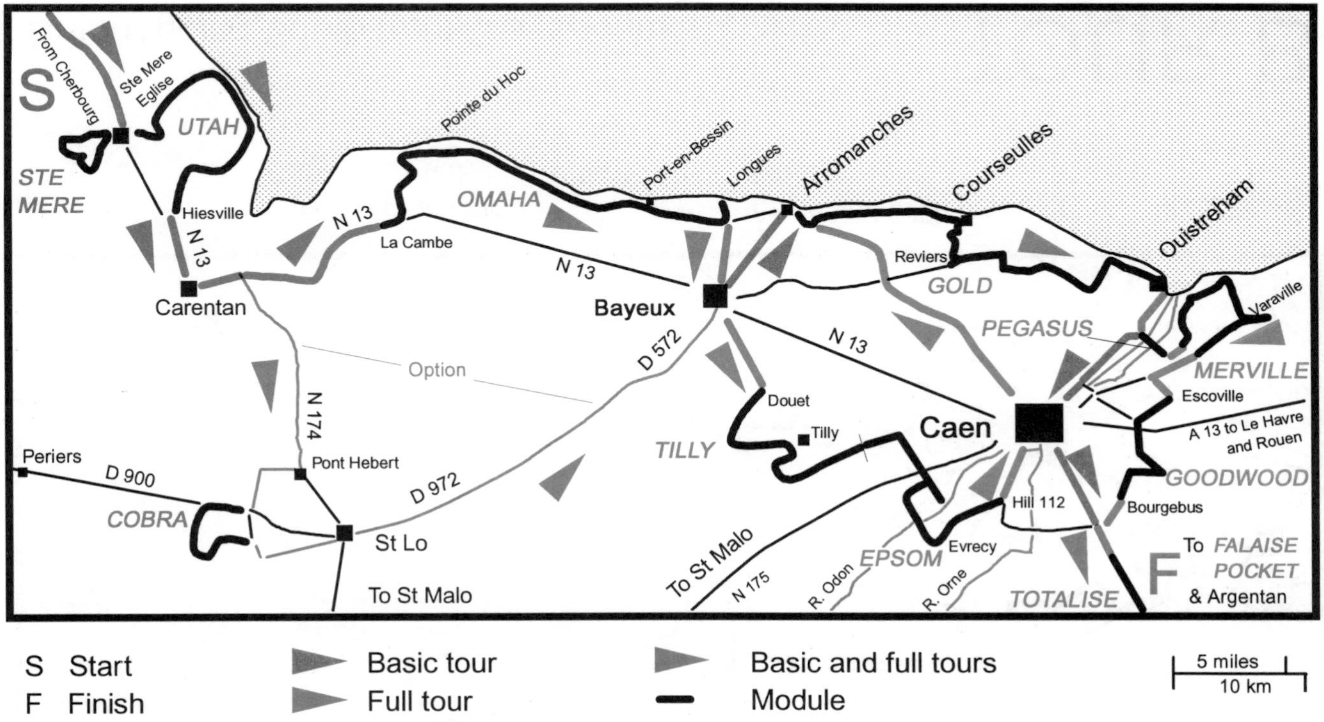

TOUR A

Detour going South from Cherbourg

Basic and full tours
▲ Module

▲ Basic tour
▲ Full tour

S Start
F Finish

5 miles
10 km

Map labels:
Ouistreham
Veyville
MERVILLE
Escoville
A 13 to Le Havre and Rouen
GOODWOOD
Bourgebus
To FALAISE POCKET
& Argentan
F
TOTALISE
PEGASUS
Hill 112
GOLD
Courseulles
Reviers
Caen
Evrecy
R. Orne
EPSOM
Arromanches
N 13
R. Odon
Longues
Port-en-Bessin
Douet
Tilly
TILLY
To St Malo
N 175
Bayeux
D 572
OMAHA
N 13
Pointe du Hoc
La Cambe
Option
D 972
St Lo
To St Malo
N 13
Pont Hebert
N 174
Carentan
Hiesville
N 13
UTAH
Ste Mere Eglise
From Cherbourg
S
STE MERE
COBRA
D 900
Peries

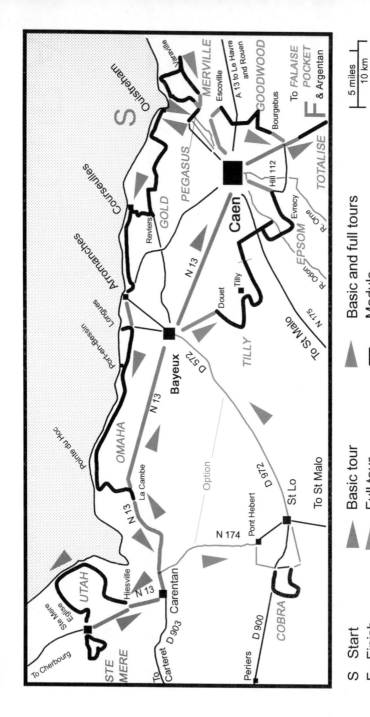

TOUR B

Detour going South from Ouistreham

S Start
F Finish

Basic and full tours
Module

Basic tour
Full tour

5 miles
10 km

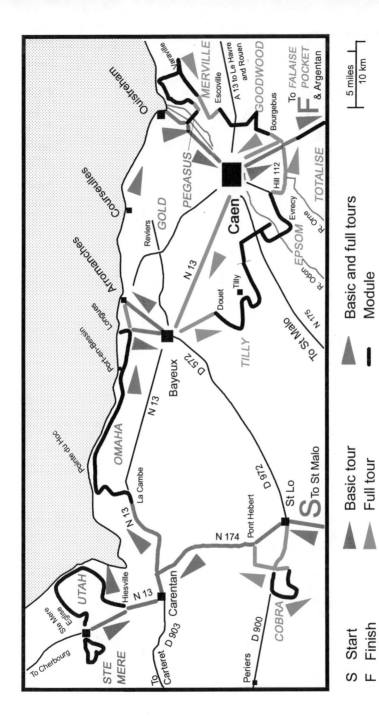

TOUR C

Detour going South from St Malo

S Start
F Finish

Basic tour
Full tour

Basic and full tours
Module

MAP C 115

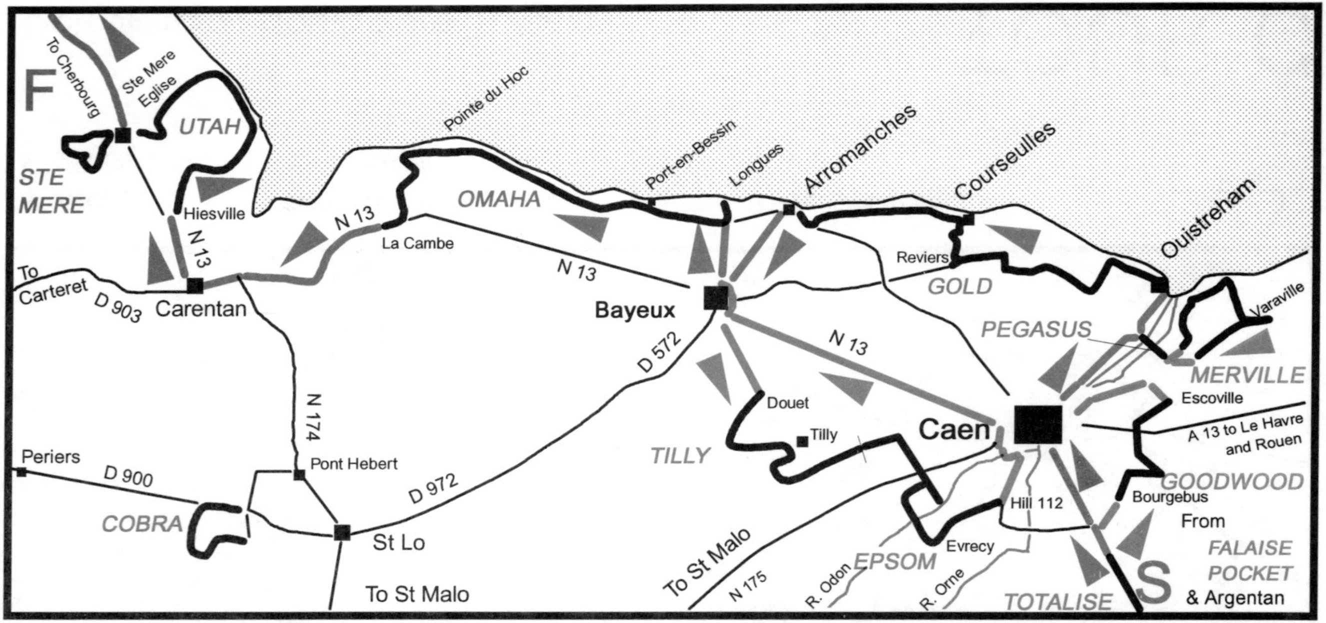

TOUR D

Detour going North to Cherbourg

Legend:

Basic and full tours
Module

▲ Basic tour
▲ Full tour

▲ Basic and full tours
— Module

S Start
F Finish

Scale: 5 miles / 10 km

Map labels:

Ouistreham, Colleville, MERVILLE, Escoville, A 13 to Le Havre and Rouen, GOODWOOD, Bourgebus, From, FALAISE POCKET, & Argentan, PEGASUS, GOLD, Courseulles, Reviers, Arromanches, Longues, Porten-bessin, Caen, Hill 112, TOTALISE, EPSOM, Evrecy, R. Orne, R. Odon, N 175, To St Malo, N 13, Douet, Tilly, TILLY, Bayeux, D 572, OMAHA, Pointe du Hoc, La Cambe, N 13, D 972, St Lo, To St Malo, N 174, Pont Hebert, Carentan, D 903, N 13, Hiesville, UTAH, Ste Mere, Eglise, To Cherbourg, STE MERE, To Carteret, D 900, Periers, COBRA

F

116 MAP D

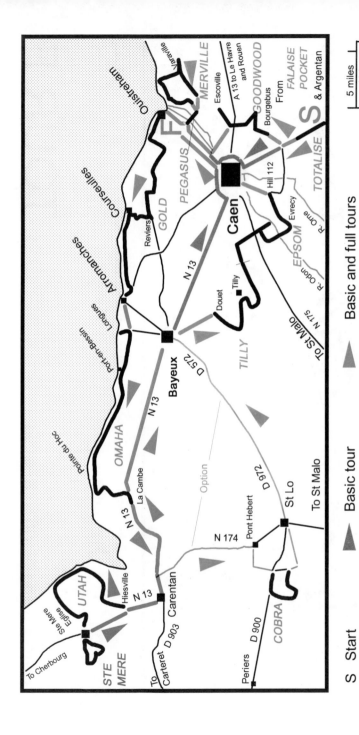

TOUR E

Detour going North to Ouistreham

S Start
F Finish

▲ Basic and full tours
▬ Module

▲ Basic tour
▲ Full tour

5 miles
10 km

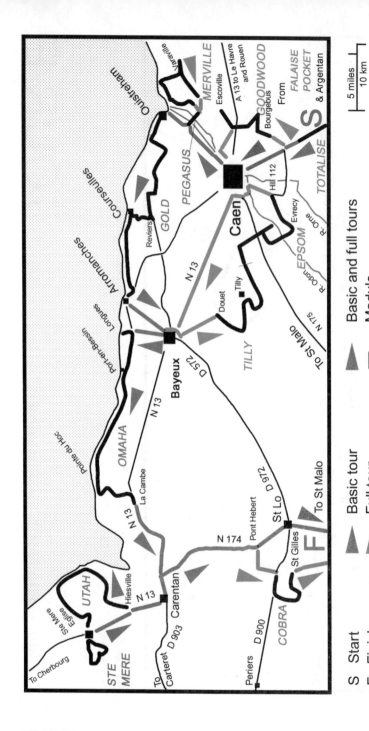

TOUR F

Detour going North to St Malo

Legend:
- ▲ Basic and full tours
- ▬ Module
- ▲ Basic tour
- ▲ Full tour
- S Start
- F Finish

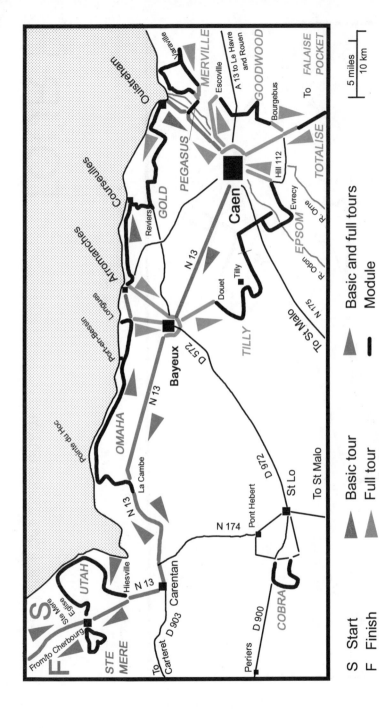

TOUR G

Circular tour from Cherbourg

S Start
F Finish

▲ Basic tour
▲ Full tour

▲ Basic and full tours
— Module

5 miles
10 km

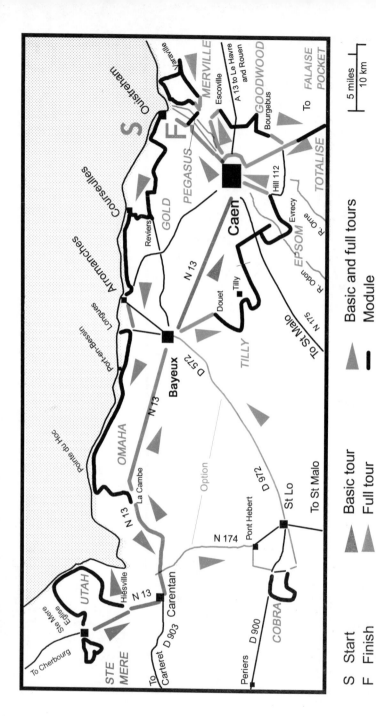

TOUR H

Circular tour from Ouistreham

S Start
F Finish

▲▲ Basic tour
▲▲ Full tour

▲ Basic and full tours
▬ Module

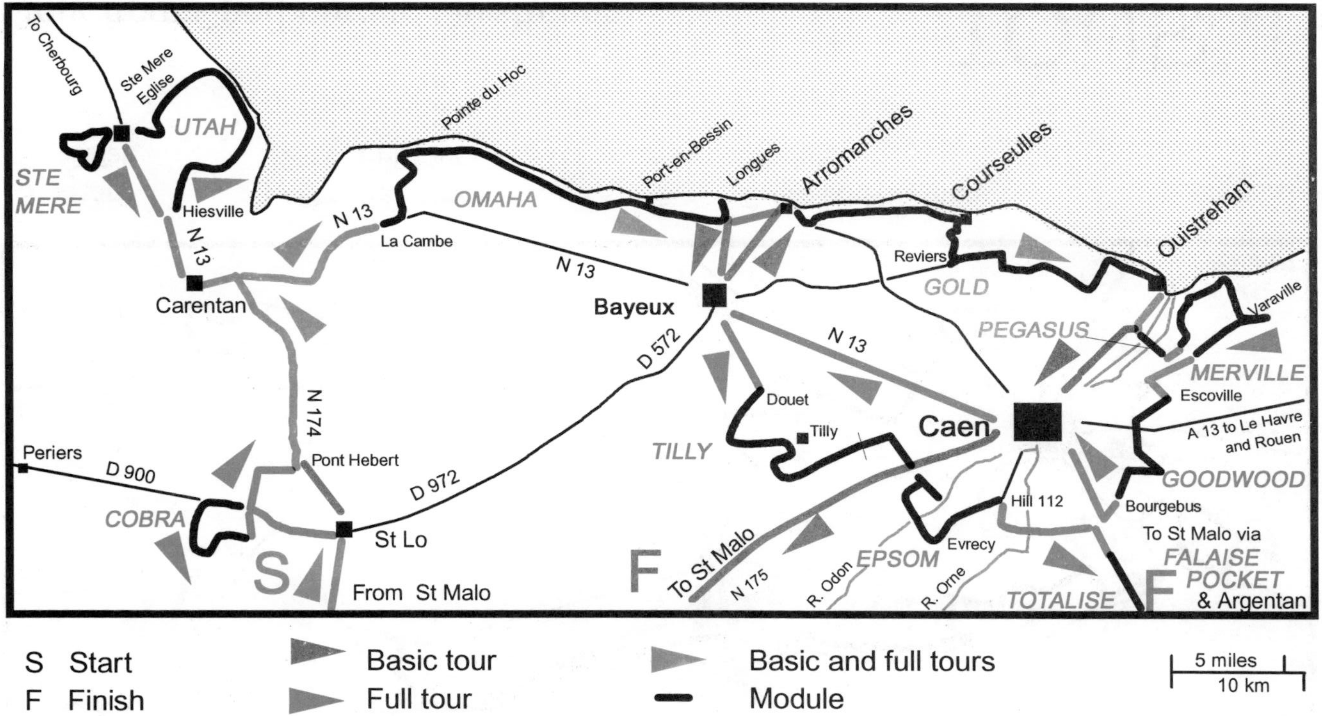

TOUR I

Circular tour from St Malo

Map legend:

- ▲ Basic and full tours
- — Module
- ▲ Basic tour
- ▲ Full tour
- S Start
- F Finish

Scale: 5 miles / 10 km

MAP I 121

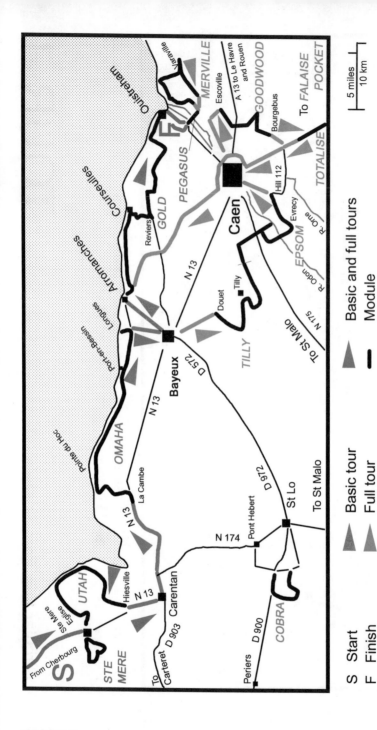

TOUR J

Tour from Cherbourg to Ouistreham

Basic and full tours ▲
Module ▬

Basic tour ▲
Full tour ▲

S Start
F Finish

5 miles
10 km

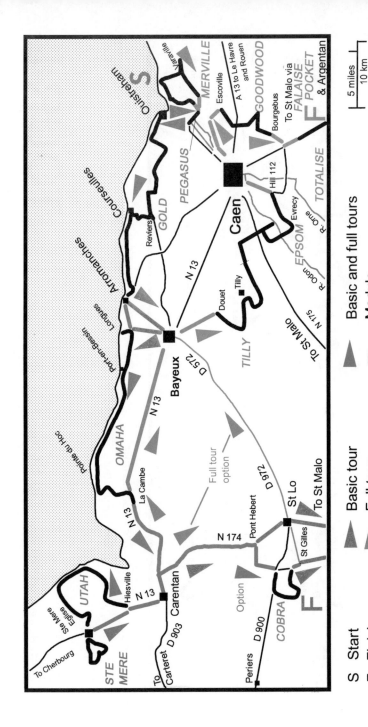

TOUR K

Tour from Ouistreham to St Malo

Legend:
- Basic and full tours
- Module
- Basic tour
- Full tour
- S Start
- F Finish

5 miles / 10 km

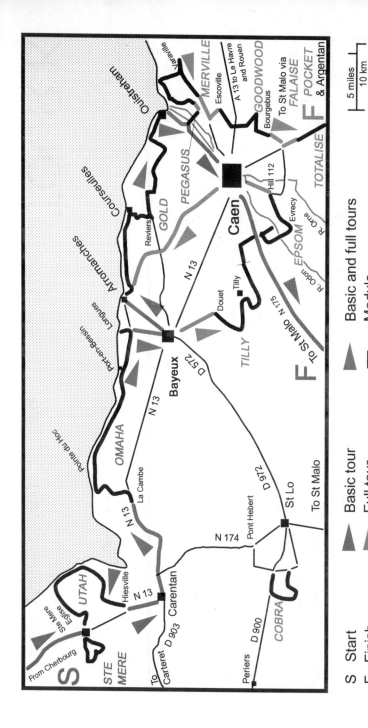

TOUR L

Tour from Cherbourg to St Malo

Legend:
- S Start
- F Finish
- Basic tour
- Full tour
- Basic and full tours
- Module

Map labels:
Ouistreham, Merville, Escoville, A 13 to Le Havre and Rouen, Goodwood, Bourgebus, To St Malo via Falaise, Pocket & Argentan, Totalise, Pegasus, Gold, Courseulles, Reviers, Caen, Hill 112, Evrecy, Epsom, R. Odon, R. Orme, Arromanches, Longues, Port-en-Bessin, Tilly, Douet, N 13, To St Malo N 175, Bayeux, D 572, Omaha, La Cambe, N 13, Pointe du Hoc, D 972, St Lo, To St Malo, N 174, Pont Hebert, Cobra, D 900, Periers, Carentan, D 903, N 13, Hiesville, Utah, Ste Mere Eglise, Ste Mere, From Cherbourg, To Carteret

5 miles / 10 km

YOUR COMMENTS

To: Easiguides,
       72 Froxfield Green, Petersfield, Hants GU32 1DQ.

From: (optional):
       Name:

       Address:

Date:

Tour followed: Code letter ....   Basic or full ....

Comments, recommendations for improvement, correction of facts, etc. - for consideration for the next edition:

continued overleaf

Thank you for taking the time to complete this.

YOUR COMMENTS CONTINUED